KU-114-660

GOLF COURSES AND COUNTRY CLUBS

GOLF COURSES AND COUNTRY CLUBS:
A GUIDE TO APPRAISAL, MARKET ANALYSIS, DEVELOPMENT, AND FINANCING

by Arthur E. Gimmy, MAI
and Martin E. Benson, MAI

**APPRAISAL
INSTITUTE**
Appraisal Institute
875 North Michigan Ave
Chicago, Illinois 60611-1980

Acknowledgments

Vice President of Publications: Christopher Bettin
Manager, Book Development: Michael R. Milgrim
Editor: Stephanie Shea-Joyce
Manager, Design/Production: Mary Jo Krysinski

For Educational Purposes Only

The opinions and statements set forth herein reflect the viewpoint of the Appraisal Institute at the time of publication but do not necessarily reflect the viewpoint of each individual member. While a great deal of care has been taken to provide accurate and current information, neither the Appraisal Institute nor its editors and staff assume responsibility for the accuracy of the data contained herein. Further, the general principles and conclusions presented in this text are subject to local, state and federal laws and regulations, court cases and any revisions of the same. This publication is sold for educational purposes with the understanding that the publisher is not engaged in rendering legal, accounting or any other professional service.

Nondiscrimination Policy

The Appraisal Institute advocates equal opportunity and nondiscrimination in the appraisal profession and conducts its activities without regard to race, color, sex, religion, national origin, or handicap status.

Library of Congress Cataloging-in-Publication Data

Gimmy, Arthur E.
    Golf courses and country clubs : a guide to appraisal, market
analysis, development, and financing / by Arthur E. Gimmy and Martin
E. Benson.
      p.   cm.
    Includes bibliographical references (p. 157) and index.
    ISBN 0-922154-05-8
    1. Golf courses--Valuation--United States.   2. Country clubs-
-Valuation--United States.   3. Golf courses--United States--Finance.
    4. Country clubs--United States--Finance.   I. Benson, Martin E.
    II. Title.
GV975.G56 1992   92-4837
796.352′06′91--dc20   CIP

TABLE OF CONTENTS

FOREWORD

Throughout the world, the golf industry is expanding. No longer the exclusive pastime of the elite, the game of golf now appeals to individuals of all ages and socioeconomic backgrounds. Over the past 50 years, the popularity of the sport has steadily increased and, in recent years, foreign and domestic investment in golf facilities has skyrocketed.

The appraisal of a golf course presents unique challenges because it involves the valuation of real estate, personal property, and a complex business. Appraisers performing such assignments must have a rudimentary understanding of the game of golf as well as a knowledge of statistics, economics, design, and legal and environmental concerns. A golf course is more than well-manicured greens and a package of amenities, it is a big business with income, expenses, and the need for wise, active management.

Appraisers interested in this valuation specialty will find in this text clear descriptions of the various types of courses (regulation length, executive, and par-3) and their operational categories (daily fee, municipal, and private). Other topics discussed include supply and demand relationships, financial feasibility, highest and best use, the application of the cost, income, and sales comparison approaches, and the problems encountered in obtaining financing. Golf courses and country clubs designed as part of residential real estate developments are covered in depth.

I am pleased to present this text and wish to thank its authors for sharing their insights into this important appraisal specialty.

Patricia J. Marshall, MAI
1992 President
Appraisal Institute

ACKNOWLEDGMENTS

The authors wish to thank the many golf course owners, managers, lenders, developers, and association staff who devoted their time and resources to providing the invaluable material contained in this text. Their collective experience is reflected throughout the book.

We also wish to thank the word processing staff of Arthur Gimmy International for their contribution to this effort. Additional appreciation and credit is due to the National Golf Foundation and the Publications Committee of the Appraisal Institute.

Arthur E. Gimmy, MAI
Martin E. Benson, MAI

ABOUT THE AUTHORS

Arthur E. Gimmy, MAI, is president and owner of Arthur Gimmy International, a nationwide real estate appraisal and consulting firm based in San Francisco, California. Mr. Gimmy has had extensive experience in valuation counseling and has given expert testimony on numerous types of property since 1960. He has a bachelor's degree in business education and a master's degree in education from the University of California in Los Angeles. In addition to his membership in the Appraisal Institute, Gimmy is a member and past president of Valuation Network, Inc., a national consortium of leading appraisal firms in the United States. Arthur Gimmy has contributed to *The Appraisal Journal* and other professional publications and is the author of *Fitness, Racquet Sports, and Spa Projects* and *Elderly Housing: A Guide to Appraisal, Market Analysis, Development, and Financing,* published in 1989 and 1988, respectively, by the Appraisal Institute. Since the 1970s Gimmy has appraised golf facilities throughout the United States, including many noteworthy PGA-rated golf courses, tropical resorts, and country clubs. He is also a frequent lecturer and author on the appraisal and analysis of golf properties.

Martin E. Benson, MAI, is vice president of Arthur Gimmy International as well as general appraisal manager and director of its Golf Properties Division. Mr. Benson has performed appraisals, feasibility studies, and market analyses on a wide variety of commercial and special-purpose properties. Since beginning his golf appraisal specialty in 1986, he has completed assignments on an extensive number of golf facilities, both existing and proposed, in many states of the nation. Prior to his appraisal career, Benson was marketing manager with a Fortune 500 corporation, an environmental science consultant, and owner of a mergers and acquisitions consulting firm. He also spent many years working in his family's residential development business. Mr. Benson holds a bachelor's degree in chemistry from San Francisco State University and a master's of business administration degree from Boston University.

INTRODUCTION

This text should provide its readers with everything they need to know about the economic characteristics of golf courses and the factors to be considered in their valuation. The information it contains will prove valuable to market analysts, developers, and lenders as well as real estate appraisers and analysts.

The first chapter of the book provides a broad overview of the game of golf, the characteristics of its players, and the nature of golf facilities. The chapters that follow explore specific subjects relating to the analysis of existing and proposed golf courses and country clubs.

Chapter 2 focuses on the facilities and components of golf courses. Factors essential to the description and analysis of the land and physical facilities are covered, including everything from site analysis to development criteria. Data on structures are provided with emphasis on clubhouses.

Chapter 3 examines the golf player and provides data on a variety of golfer characteristics. It explores why people play or don't play golf, divides golfers into behavioral categories, provides information on the varying levels of playing skill, and includes information on golf expenditures, instruction, and travel.

Chapter 4 brings together demographic data, supply considerations, and demand factors to describe the process in which market potential and trends are analyzed.

In the analysis of a proposed golf facility, whether it is an entirely new project or an expansion, all the elements of design, cost, supply, demand, income, and expenses must be expressed and summarized. Chapter 5 offers a practical approach to determining a facility's financial feasibility. The application of internal rate of return analysis is explained and conclusions are drawn relative to a proposed facility's future performance and market acceptance.

In Chapters 6 through 9, traditional valuation approaches are applied to profit-oriented golf courses or country clubs. Chapter 6 describes the determination of highest and best use and the factors that must be considered. Chapter 7 explores the cost approach and provides the methodology for preparing a separate estimate of the business component of the enterprise. Typical and unusual land valuation practices are explained. Chapter 8 covers the income approach and explains all the components of a golf course investment that should be reflected in the net income projection. The discounting and capitalization of income to derive the overall value of the assets is described by application of direct capitalization and discounted cash flow analysis techniques. The allocation of a value to each component of the investment is also explained. The sales comparison approach is the subject of Chapter 9, in which valuation units are identified and adjustment factors and grids are utilized.

Nonprofit golf clubs and courses developed and operated to enhance real estate lot sales represent a separate and extremely difficult appraisal challenge. In Chapter 10 all three approaches to valuation are applied to this common appraisal situation. Other specialized valuation topics covered include trophy courses, eminent domain, tax assessment, leaseholds, and price segregation.

Chapter 11 examines the financing problems that may confront the valuer or economic consultant. The data presented were gathered from a survey of lenders conducted by the authors of this text. The subjects discussed include financing terms, lending requirements, and appraisal critiques.

Many golf course appraisal assignments involve the surrounding land, which may be a residential community or resort project. The unique considerations and valuation factors that relate to this type of golf course are identified and analyzed in Chapter 12.

In Chapter 13 the findings of the authors' research and recommendations are summarized. Conclusions are presented concerning the future of golfing and the analysis of a golf course business. Unique valuation problems that will continue to challenge analysts in this field are explored, and predictions for the future of the industry are presented as they relate to development, feasibility, and valuation.

CHAPTER ONE

DEVELOPMENT OF GOLF AND GOLF COURSES

BACKGROUND AND HISTORY

A golf course is a unique challenge, whether one is a player, developer, lender, or appraiser. The game of golf and the appraisal of golf course facilities can be difficult and vexing. Golf was designed to provide relaxation and opportunity for social interaction and exercise, but for some it represents a complete lifestyle. Golf is an extremely popular sport and tremendous growth is taking place in the industry.

To the uninitiated, a golf course is a large piece of land lightly populated by brightly dressed people riding in golf cars or hauling bags of clubs. To those involved in its operation, development, design, or analysis, a golf course is a complicated enterprise representing an investment in real estate, personal property, inventory, people, and goodwill.

For valuation purposes, a golf course or country club must be considered a business, not an assemblage of physical assets. The analyst of such a property must possess unique skills: a knowledge of statistics, economics, design, and management and the ability to value real estate, personal property, and a business operation. These qualifications may appear overwhelming, but they can be satisfied through the cooperation of two or more specialists. Knowledge of the sport is a prerequisite, but extensive golfing skill is not.

Readers of this text will be rewarded with new knowledge and insights into the sport of golf. A first step is to understand the history of the game.

AN ANCIENT SPORT

Golf is native to Scotland, where it probably originated in the 15th century. "A major role-player of the day was King James II of Scotland, whom we can thank for our first reference to the game, as he decreed in 1457 that citizens should desist from playing golf."[1]

The popularity of the game gradually increased as courses were built and equipment was improved. A golf course at St. Andrews, Scotland, is known as the cradle of the royal game.

The evolution of golf can be seen in the composition of golf balls. Changes in the game fall into four eras: use of featherie golf balls (1620–1850), gutta percha balls (1851–1900), rubber core golf balls (1901–1960), and hard core balls, which were introduced in 1961.

EARLY DEVELOPMENT IN THE UNITED STATES

Golf spread through the world as Scots emigrated from their native land and brought the game with them. The game had an early impact on the United

1. Richard E. Donovan and Joseph S. F. Murdock, *The Game of Golf and the Printed Word* (Endicott, N.Y.: Castalio Press, 1988), xii.

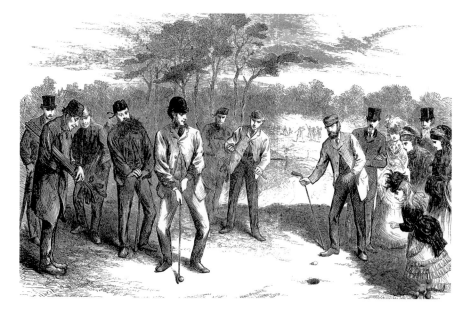

▶
Golf was a
gentlemen's game.

States, where courses for the leisure class were founded along the Atlantic seaboard beginning in 1780. A pamphlet written in 1772 provides an early description of the sport. "Golf is an exercise which is much used by the Gentlemen in Scotland. A large common in which there are several little holes is chosen for the purpose. It is played with little leather balls fluffed with feathers; and sticks made somewhat in the form of handy-wicket. He who puts a ball into a given number of holes, with the fewest strokes, gets the game."[2]

In 1887 the first permanent golf club and course was established at Foxburg, Pennsylvania. In the following year the first golf association was formed. In 1894 the Amateur Golf Association was created to establish uniform rules and conduct tournaments. Golf courses were developed by private clubs, colleges, and universities, mostly in the Northeast. By the end of the nineteenth century, approximately 950 golf courses existed in the United States, with at least one in each state.[3] (For more details on the history of golf in the United States, refer to the bibliography.)

GOLF COURSE CONSTRUCTION

As illustrated in Figure 1.1, golf course construction in the United States has gone through distinct phases. There were approximately 1,000 courses in the early years of the century, but the number declined during World War I. In the Roaring Twenties, there was unparalleled growth, with approximately 550 new courses built each year between 1923 and 1931. A great golfer named Bobby Jones epitomized this period, which is sometimes referred to as the Golden Age of Sport.

During the Depression and World War II, golf course construction virtually stopped due to bad economic times. In fact, there was a decline in the total number of facilities until 1946. Activity was sluggish in postwar years, but after President Eisenhower's golfing endeavors were widely publicized, golf course construction surged.

Beginning in the 1950s televised golf made stars of Arnold Palmer, Ben

2. Ibid, iv.

3. Robert L. A. Adams and John F. Rooney Jr., "Evolution of American Golf Facilities," *Geographical Review*, vol. 75, no. 4 (October 1985), 422.

FIGURE 1.1 NUMBER OF U.S. GOLF COURSES

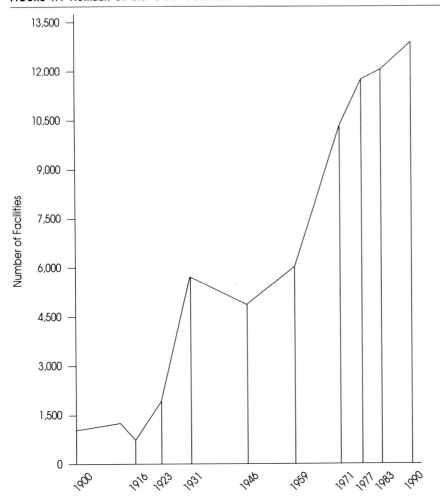

Source: Cornish and Whitten, *The Golf Course*; Adams and Rooney, "Evolution of American Golf Facilities"; National Golf Foundation

Hogan, Billy Casper, Sam Snead, Jack Nicklaus, and others. Residential development with golf courses as the key amenity created explosive popularity for golf between 1959 and 1971. During this period a large number of nine-hole courses were developed.

From the mid-1970s through the mid-1980s, between 100 and 150 new courses opened each year. The popularity of golf continued to grow, despite two recessions, unprecedented high interest rates and tight money. Now golf has entered a new phase of strong demand fueled by demographics and the recreational needs of a growing and aging population.

Since 1985, the number of people who play golf has increased by more than eight million; in 1989 and 1990 almost 300 new courses opened annually. The increase in the number of golfers reflects both the increasing population and a rising participation rate. In 1986 one out of every 11 adult Americans played some golf; in 1990, the figure was closer to one in eight.

Most areas have a serious shortage of golf facilities. Some experts estimate that a new course would have to be added to the national inventory every day during the 1990s to meet existing demand. The outlook continues to be positive even though commercial mortgage money is tight. In early 1991, 560 courses were under construction and 781 were being planned.[4]

4. *Golf Facilities in the United States* (Jupiter, Fla.: National Golf Foundation, 1991).

TABLE 1.1 U.S. AGE WAVE AND GOLF, 1990

Category	5–17	18–29	30–39	40–49	50–59	60–64	65+	Totals
U.S. population (millions)	46	47	42	32	22	11	32	232
Participation rate (% who are golfers)	5.8	16.5	16.3	13.9	12.2	11.8	8.5	12.2
No. of golfers (millions)	2.7	7.8	6.9	4.5	2.7	1.2	2.7	28.5
Frequency rate (No. of rounds played per year per golfer)	10.0	11.6	12.7	17.0	23.9	36.5	43.2	17.8
Total rounds (millions)	2.7	90	87	76	65	44	117	506

Source: National Golf Foundation

The demographic and recreational trends affecting the U.S. market are fueling a similar, large-scale expansion of golf projects in Great Britain, Germany, France, Belgium, Spain, and Sweden. Even the USSR is getting into the act; a new golf course opened there in the spring of 1991.

WHO PLAYS GOLF

Golf is now marketed and priced to attract all age groups. As shown in Table 1.1, the largest percentage of players are in the 18- to 29-year-old age group, where one in six individuals plays golf. This does not mean, however, that young adults dominate the sport. Fewer older people are playing golf, only 9% of those over 60, but these individuals play far more frequently. As a result, approximately the same number of rounds per year are played by players ranging in age from 18 to 39 years and those 60 years old and older.

In all age groups golf participation is approximately three and a half times greater among males (19.4%) than females (5.6%). However, the number of women golfers is increasing more rapidly.

Golf is perceived to be an expensive sport because of its association with private clubs. Advertisers use a country club atmosphere to sell high-priced cars, perfume, and clothing. In reality, playing golf regularly at a municipal course is not much more costly than membership in an upscale health or racquet sport facility.

Nevertheless, past golf participation is directly related to household income. In 1990, 22.2% of players came from households with incomes over $75,000, 17.7% from the $50,000 to $74,999 income category, 15.5% from the $40,000 to $49,999 category, 11.8% from the $30,000 to $39,999 category, 10.5% from the $20,000 to $29,999 category, and 6.5% from the $10,000 to $19,999 category.

There are some surprises in the occupations of golfers. As expected, professionals and managers account for a very large portion (45.8%) of all golfers, but blue collar workers now account for 27% of all golfers. Clerical and sales workers represent 18.3% of the total, followed by retired persons and others at 8.9%.

Statistical information on the demographic profile of golfers by participation rate and region is included in Chapter 4. More detailed data may be obtained from the National Golf Foundation.

TYPES OF GOLF COURSES

A typical course has either nine or 18 holes, each consisting of a tee, a fairway, and a green. The objective of the game, and the measure of the golfer's skill, is to move the golf ball from the tee into the hole on the green using the least number of strokes over the total number of holes played. Players compete by comparing their scores with those of their competitors or associates and against *par*, the number of strokes that an expert golfer could be expected to achieve on a given hole or series of holes.

Par allows the golfer two putts after the ball is on the green. Thus, a par-3 hole allows for one shot plus two putts, a par-4 hole allows for two shots and two putts, and a par-5 allows for three shots and two putts. Par is computed solely on distance (see Table 1.2).

TABLE 1.2 DISTANCE IN YARDS

Par	Men	Women
3	Up to 250	Up to 210
4	251 to 470	211 to 400
5	471 and over	401 and over

Source: National Golf Foundation. *Planning and Building a Golf Course* (Jupiter, Fla.: National Golf Foundation, 1985), 9.

It is an oversimplification to refer to a golf course as "typical" when describing it for analytical purposes. Golf courses can be identified by their size, type of operational category, economic motivation, layout, topography, location, and difficulty, or by other characteristics. An understanding of these categories is necessary before any type of analysis can be undertaken.

Size

There are three basic types of courses: regulation, executive, and par-3.

Regulation courses, the traditional type, are the most popular. An 18-hole course should have a par, or difficulty rating, of 72 and a length of 6,300 to 6,700 yards. The effective length from various tees can range from 5,200 to 7,200 yards. (This subject will be discussed in Chapter 2.) Par ranges from three to five strokes per hole. The basic mix of holes for a par 72 course is 10 par-4s, four par-3s, and four par-5s. A course with a par of 70 or 71 is acceptable if the size of the property or nature of the terrain prevents the designing of four good par-5 holes. Total par should always be reduced by replacing one or two par-5s with par-4s. A regulation course should always have four par-3s.[5]

Executive courses are thought of as shorter regulation courses. They can be designed in limited areas and usually range in size from 40 to 75 acres with a length of 3,000 to 4,500 yards. Par ratings are generally between 58 to 68, allowing for a mixture of mostly par-3 and par-4 holes. Executive courses can provide the challenge of a regulation course in much less playing time.

In a par-3 course each hole has a par-3 rating for a total par of 54. The typical hole ranges from 75 to 240 yards and the total yardage is 2,000 to 2,500. These courses have a total area of 35 to 45 acres. Par-3 courses may be adjuncts to regulation courses, driving ranges, and resorts, or stand-alone operations. They can be sized downward to "pitch and putt" layouts, requiring as little as 10 acres with holes less than 100 yards in length. Such courses are played with as few as two clubs: a pitching iron or wedge and a putter.

5. *Planning and Building a Golf Course* (Jupiter, Fla.: National Golf Foundation, 1985), 8.

Golf courses are sometimes broadly categorized as regulation-sized or short courses. Short courses (executive and par-3 types) are popular because of their shorter playing time and lower green fees. Developers and operators like the reduced land area and lower construction, operating, and maintenance costs.

Golf courses can vary in total size from nine holes to 27, 36, 45, 54, 72, or 90 holes. Nine-hole courses account for 40% of all golf courses in the United States. They are typically developed on sites with limited acreage. A regulation nine-hole course can have a par of 35 or 36 and range from 3,000 to 3,400 yards. To play a full round, the golfer tours the course twice. An executive nine-hole course is smaller, with a total length of 1,500 to 2,300 yards and a par between 29 and 33. It typically has a par of 33 with one par-5, four par-4, and four par-3 holes.

Operational Category

Virtually all statistics for golf facilities recognize three operational categories: private, daily fee, and municipal. These broad groupings must be further described.

Private Courses

Membership in a private club is very limited and usually expensive. The course is closed to the general public except for guest and special groups; members usually have lifetime tenure and pay monthly dues. Memberships are acquired by paying an initiation fee or purchasing a membership from another member. Private courses may or may not be operated as profit-making ventures.

Daily-Fee Courses

The largest and fastest growing category is the daily fee course. This broad category includes courses owned and operated for and available to the general public. Some users may hold memberships while nonmembers pay a daily fee.

Municipal Courses

Municipal courses are owned by government entities such as cities, counties, and the armed forces. They are the fewest in number, and are operated on a daily-fee basis. Government agencies may operate on a nonprofit basis or lease courses to private corporations, individuals, and concessionaires who manage them to produce a profit.

In 1990 there were 13,951 golf courses in the United States. Table 1.3 provides statistics on their size and operational characteristics.

TABLE 1.3 TYPES OF COURSES BY COURSE LENGTH AND OPERATIONAL CATEGORY (1990)

Length	Daily Fee	Municipal	Private	Total
Regulation	5,529	1,926	4,948	12,403
Executive	507	139	162	808
Par-3	461	157	122	740
Totals	6,497	2,222	5,232	13,951

Source: National Golf Foundation. *Golf Facilities in the U.S., 1991 Edition* (Jupiter, Fla.: National Golf Foundation, 1991).

Economic Motivation

Golf course ownership can be profit-seeking or nonprofit. A course operated for profit is an investment that can be valued by applying accepted appraisal techniques and approaches. The typical characteristics of such a course include availability to the public, maximization of rounds, and inclusion of various departments (e.g., pro shop, driving range, restaurant) for the profitable sale of goods and services.

Nonprofit courses are operated for their amenities, not for monetary returns. A comparison with residential property clarifies this distinction. The benefits derived from home ownership include the provision of shelter and a setting for social activities and recreation. A nonprofit golf course provides some of the same amenities. A house produces no income, but it has value to the owner; similarly a nonprofit golf course has value to its members or the community because it yields returns in the form of amenities rather than money.

The many factors to be considered in the appraisal of nonprofit courses are discussed in Chapter 10.

Layout

A regulation-sized course may be designed in one of five basic configurations:

1. Core course
2. Single-fairway, continuous 18-hole course
3. Single-fairway, 18-hole course with returning nines
4. Double-fairway, continuous 18-hole course
5. Double-fairway, 18-hole course with returning nines

These five layouts are illustrated in Figure 1.2.

Statistics on golf course design are not available, but core golf courses are preferred because they require the least amount of land, usually between 110 and 140 acres. Other layouts generally require 140 to 175 acres. Short courses can be designed with a single loop, double fairway, or core layout.

Topography

Golf courses can also be categorized by the type of terrain.

- Flat courses laid out on valley land.
- Gently sloping courses, which may be located in floodplains.
- Hilly courses on gently rolling to moderately sloping hillsides and valleys.

Flat courses have the lowest development costs followed by gently sloping courses. Hilly courses are the most expensive to develop.

Location

Golf courses are found in a variety of settings, each with its own characteristics. Suitable locations include, but are not limited to, residential subdivisions, resorts, country clubs, and parks and open space. Golf courses are frequently designed for maximum exposure to residential lots because a golf course can enhance property value.

Difficulty

Golf courses range from highly landscaped, fully turfed courses to rough links courses, with many variations in between these two extremes. The cost and playability of a golf course depend to a great extent on design factors.

FIGURE 1.2 GOLF COURSE LAYOUTS

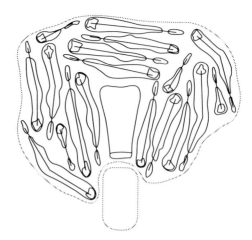

Core golf course

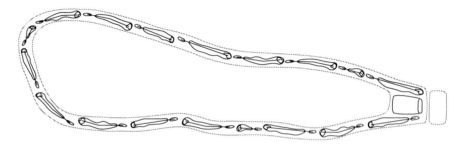

Single-fairway, continuous, 18-hole course

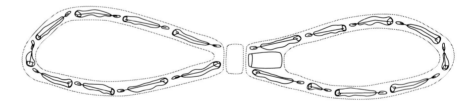

Single-fairway, 18-hole course with returning nines

Double-fairway, continuous, 18-hole course

Double-fairway, 18-hole course with returning nines

Source: Urban Land Institute

These factors contribute to the difficulty of a course: tee placement, length, green size, hole visibility, contour, hazards, and climatic condition such as prevailing winds.

The difficulty of a course should match its market. Resort courses are typically more difficult to play than courses oriented to older players. The former are designed to challenge serious, accomplished golfers with greater length and more hazards; the latter are likely to be characterized by shorter distances, easier greens, and multiple-position tees.

BUSINESS OPERATIONS

A golf course or country club rarely represents a single revenue source or operating entity. Table 1.4 shows the distribution of major characteristics among various types of courses.

TABLE 1.4 GOLF COURSE CHARACTERISTICS

Characteristic	Regulation	Pitch & Putt	Par-3	Executive
Size				
18 holes	A	D	D	B
9 holes	A	B	B	D
Operational category				
Private membership	C	E	E	D
Daily fee	C	A	A	A
Municipal	D	D	B	B
Economic motivation				
Profit-seeking	B	B	C	B
Nonprofit	D	D	C	D
Location				
Residential subdivisions	B	E	D	B
Resorts	B	D	D	B
Country clubs	A	D	D	D
Parks or open space	B	D	C	C
Related facilities				
Driving range	B	E	D	C
Pro shop	A	D	D	B
Clubhouse	A	E	D	B
Car rentals	A	E	E	C
Restaurant & lounge	B	E	E	C
Snack bar	A	B	A	A
Health and fitness facilities	D	E	E	D

Legend:
A – denotes that the characteristic specified is always included in this type of course
B – characteristic usually included
C – characteristic included in 50% of golf courses of this type
D – characteristic seldom included
E – characteristic never included

EXAMPLE: The table indicates that a par-3 course usually has nine holes.

Many minor characteristics can also be considered. The simplest type of course might be a nine-hole municipal course with two buildings: a place to pay and receive a starting time and a maintenance building for the storage of equipment and supplies. The administration building may also provide space for the sale of snacks and balls and equipment rental. In a country club setting, the facilities may include:

- A driving range
- A pro shop selling clothing and all types of equipment

- A clubhouse that provides amenities such as lockers, showers, saunas, steam rooms, spas, and child care facilities
- Golf car rentals, including storage sheds and a maintenance shop
- Restaurant and lounge areas—e.g., coffee shop, gourmet dining room, cocktail bar, entertainment lounge
- One or more snack bars spread around the course including, perhaps, a separate facility for children and teenagers
- Health and fitness facilities such as tennis courts, racquetball and squash courts, a swimming pool, and an exercise room.

In an appraisal each income-producing department must be carefully analyzed. On the expense side there may be two to three times more operating expense categories to examine. With all these factors to consider, preparing a meaningful evaluation, market analysis, financial feasibility study, or appraisal can be a challenge for any analyst.

THE VALUATION PROCESS

The valuation process is a methodology used to solve a client's specific question about property value. This process begins with identification of the specific problem to be solved and ends when a solution is reported to the client. This process is defined and described in the Appraisal Institute's textbook *The Appraisal of Real Estate*. Figure 1.3, The Valuation Process, which illustrates this process, is taken from that text.

The valuation process shown in the figure is applicable in valuing golf courses and country clubs. In this text, the analytical structure will be specifically applied to golf facilities, addressing their unique characteristics, the valuation problems they create, and possible solutions.

All three of the fundamental approaches to value (cost, income capitalizaton, and sale comparison) are appropriate in the appraisal of golf courses and country clubs. These approaches can be properly applied to estimate the value of the real estate—i.e., all physical assets—as well as the entire facility as a going concern. Note that in the valuation of a golf facility as a going concern there can be a component of value attributable to the intangible assets of the business. These assets are commonly referred to as *goodwill* and are often divided into specialized components such as permits and licenses, name or reputation, customer lists, management systems, management contracts and covenants not to compete, staff in place, supplier relationships, golf professional agreements, and tournament contracts.

To meet the requirements of accepted appraisal standards, the values of the real estate assets must often be segregated from the personal property and the intangible aspects of the enterprise. The need to segregate value in this way is determined by the requirements of the assignment. Segregation of the various components of value is typically required for mortgage financing and property tax purposes, but it is often not necessary for feasibility analyses, investment decisions, or determining a sale price. It is, however, appropriate for allocating a sale price in terms of its associated tax implications. The procedures set forth in this book will assist readers in the analysis and valuation of all the components of a golf course or country club. (See Chapters 7 through 9.) It is the responsibility of the appraiser to determine when such separate values are required for the real estate, the personal property, and the business and to value the property components appropriately for that assignment.

FIGURE 1.3 THE VALUATION PROCESS

Definition of the Problem						
Identification of real estate	Identification of property rights to be valued	Use of appraisal	Definition of value	Date of value estimate	Description of scope of appraisal	Other limiting conditions

Preliminary Analysis and Data Selection and Collection		
General (Region, city, and neighborhood)	**Specific (Subject and comparables)**	**Competitive Supply and Demand (The subject market)**
Social	Site and improvements	Inventory of competitive
Economic	Cost and depreciation	properties
Governmental	Income/expense and	Sales and listings
Environmental	capitalization rate	Vacancies and offerings
	History of ownership	Absorption rates
	and use of property	Demand studies

Highest and Best Use Analysis
Land as though vacant
Property as improved
Specified in terms of
use, time, and market participants

Land Value Estimate

Application of the Three Approaches		
Cost	Sales comparison	Income capitalization

Reconciliation of Value Indications and Final Value Estimate

Report of Defined Value

CHAPTER TWO

THE GAME AND ITS FACILITIES

 The characteristics of a golf course site ultimately determine the type of course built and its design. In Chapter 1 five basic design options were listed: core, single-fairway continuous, single-fairway with returning nines, double-fairway continuous, and double-fairway with returning nines. Variations of these basic designs such as concentric circle or flower petal courses may be considered distinct types by some course architects.

Course design is greatly influenced by the amount of land available, the investment objectives of the real estate developers, the density of adjacent land uses, and other factors such as the investors' perception of quality, operating costs, and the need to differentiate from competitive courses.

Recognized qualitative differences between golf courses relate to playability, aesthetics, condition, reputation, and location. There are no set criteria for classifying courses qualitatively, but certain facilities are described as *trophy* or *signature* courses. A *signature course* is one that has been designed by a well-known golf course architect. A *trophy course* is a signature course with a world-class reputation, a unique location, and exceptional design and layout. Qualitative considerations influence value, but are subjective in nature. To assess qualitative factors an appraiser must examine a variety of facilities and develop the ability to evaluate critical differences.

The construction of a golf facility cannot be covered in detail in this chapter, but the reader can become acquainted with the scope of various improvements and equipment, the importance of careful design, and the functional relationships reflected in the overall operation and utilization of various parts of the property. For additional information the reader is referred to specialized texts listed in the bibliography.

For the appraiser the process of describing a golf course begins with the raw land before any improvements have been made.

SITE FEATURES

A golf course site description includes consideration of site size (acres), shape, topography, utilities (especially water), accessibility, soils, vegetation, and other factors.

Golf course sites vary greatly in size. Regulation 18-hole courses generally cover 120 to 180 acres; a range of 160 to 180 acres is typical for a 6,500-yard course on gently rolling land. Core courses require the smallest amount of land, double fairways require more, and single fairways are the least efficient. A developer who wants to include a golf course as a project amenity, but has a limited amount of land, might consider a short course ranging from a nine-hole, par-3 course built on 35 acres to an 18-hole, executive course built on 40 to 75 acres.

With the various design options that are available, the shape of sites can vary enormously. If a large parcel of land is available for a mixed project consisting of a golf course and residential lots, the investors will seek to maximize the amount of developable land along the fairways in designing the golf course. In this instance, a core course is the least desirable option. A combination of single and double fairways is typically found in golf courses attached to subdivisions. The controlling variable in the design of a course is usually topography.

The slope and contours of the terrain determine the course layout and routing plan, especially when the course is associated with adjacent building sites. Fairways should be at the same or lower elevations than housing sites to promote visibility. On undulating terrain, the course designer must determine the location of tees (on flat or cut-and-fill areas) and greens (in landing areas that are visible, not unduly hilly, and framed by natural or landscaped features). The optimal design will provide a variety of hole lengths, difficulty, and style. A combination of two par-3 holes, five par-4s, and two par-5s will yield a total par of 36 over nine holes. If they can be designed in a sequence of 4–5–4–3–4–5–4–3–4 or 4–3–4–5–4–3–4–5–4, no two consecutive holes will have the same par. This combination may be ideal, but it is atypical. The only firm criteria are that par-3 holes should not be at the beginning or end of the course and should be spaced to avoid backups.

The basic utilities required for a golf course project or country club include electricity, domestic and irrigation water, and a sanitary sewer or septic system. Because water to irrigate the course is essential, the adequacy and quality of the water supply must be thoroughly investigated and validated. Typical sources of water include local water companies; on-site wells, canals, or aqueducts; lakes or streams; and effluent from waste water treatment plants. Except for the latter source, which is becoming more acceptable, public water sources tend to be too expensive.

The availability of sufficient water may be a critical problem for proposed courses and some existing courses where climatic factors have resulted in water shortages or fluctuations in area supplies. Actual water requirements can vary greatly. An 18-hole, regulation-sized course may use between 250,000 and 500,000 gallons per day depending on the amount and type of ground cover, climatic conditions, and the means of irrigation.

The appraiser should thoroughly investigate the status of current and future water supplies, potential alternative sources, and factors that may result in future restrictions or supply interruptions. A problem is emerging in semi-arid, southwestern locations where the drawdown of underground reservoirs has endangered domestic supplies in the surrounding area.

One important positive trend is the use of treated effluent for golf course irrigation. In many cases the disposal of waste water is a problem for local sanitation districts. It can be quite cost-efficient for a golf course developer or operator to make use of this water. In some cases the ability to develop a course has hinged on the availability of treated effluent.

Soils of all types can support golf course construction, but differences in soil quality can greatly affect development costs and operating expenses. The best soils are alluvial, sandy loam types which have good drainage characteristics and support healthy turf and ground cover. Soils that are rocky, clayish, mucky, or gravelly are undesirable because they can result in drainage problems, higher construction costs, and excessive maintenance expenditures. In recent years golf courses have even been built on lava fields in Hawaii, but at great expense.

Courses are sometimes developed in floodplains and seasonal wetlands when more desirable sites are not available. The advantage of a lower land cost may be offset, however, if the course is unavailable during rainy periods, and maintenance costs are high. Design features such as crowned fairways and drainage systems can overcome many of the problems of low-lying land and improve the appearance of a property.

Geographic conditions in the U.S. divide golf course locations into two general categories: Frostbelt and Sunbelt. The length of the playing season in these locations can vary by several months, which affects the number of rounds played and the projects' income and expense performance.

This general discussion of site characteristics is only a starting point for the serious analyst. Many factors must be considered in selecting and describing a golf course site. Site factors can play an important role in the estimation of land value and in any comparisons made between golf course sales and a subject property. Sources of additional data are listed in the bibliography.

COURSE CHARACTERISTICS

Golf courses are designed to meet the requirements of a specific market or markets. Typical or desirable features for regulation courses designed for specific markets can be described.

Municipal Courses

The simplest of courses, municipal golf courses, are designed to accommodate heavy daily play throughout the year or season and to appeal to a wide variety of players. Typically a core design is used with emphasis on playability and enough complexity to challenge a wide range of players. These courses tend to be flat and have few rough areas where balls can be lost. Development and operating costs are typically low due to the concentration of the irrigation system, easy mowing, reduced landscape maintenance, and fewer obstacles. Municipal courses are shorter than most (approximately 6,000 to 6,500 yards) and fairways are wide.

Resort Courses

Resort courses are the most complicated type of courses. They are designed to appeal to serious golfers, but also serve as a marketing tool to attract a broader market of group and convention business. Resort courses are distinguished by memorable holes, scenic beauty, a feeling of privacy or spaciousness, "signature" designers of course architects, lakes, and a variety of hazards. They usually feature a core or double-fairway layout and have high construction and maintenance costs.

Retirement Community Courses

The typical player at a retirement community course is older, but plays often, so the course should not be situated in difficult terrain. These courses are shorter, have wide fairways for faster play, and are challenging in terms of visibility and the placement of hazards. Retirement community courses range from 5,500 to 6,500 yards in length. They may have a single- or double-fairway layout to maximize frontage along surrounding land and be easy to maintain.

In addition to these three basic course types, desirable characteristics may be combined to produce hybrids and variations. For example, a semi-private course in a residential setting might include features to attract a wide market without compromising design features and the need for challenging holes. Where land is available and market dynamics warrant it, a 27-hole course can be built to provide three distinct, 18-hole combinations designed to appeal to players of varying expertise. Generally, 27-hole facilities increase golf course capacity by two-thirds, but are only 50% more expensive to develop.

DESCRIBING THE COURSE

To describe and analyze a golf course for valuation purposes, an understanding of its functional parts is needed. A typical hole includes a tee, fairway, green, rough, and hazards (see Figure 2.1). These elements are combined in different ways to form unique golf courses. Once the appraiser has a basic understanding of golf courses, he or she can develop the ability to describe them, critique them, compare them, and rate them through practice and exposure to a variety of facilities.

Tees

As the starting point for each hole, a tee must be carefully placed and sized. Because tee shots generally range from 150 to 250 yards, it is desirable to have three or four sets of tees at varying downhill locations to meet the needs of a wide range of golfers. The tees are spaced over a distance of approximately 50 to 75 yards and identified as gold (for a drive of 250 yards), blue (for a drive of 225 yards), white (for a drive of 175 yards), and red (for a drive of 150 yards). A good design relates the overall size of tees to the number of annual rounds; there is a direct relationship between the amount of play and tee damage or wear and tear. A general rule of thumb is 100 to 200 square feet of tee surface for each 1,000 rounds played per year. Tees should be level and planted with sturdy turf.

Designing a tee requires careful consideration of a number of factors: proper soil and drainage, adequate exposure to sunshine and air movement, limited slope for mowing purposes, and appropriate fairway orientation to minimize damage to adjacent property from errant drives.

Tees are subject to a great deal of hard use and need constant attention. When they are sized properly, the tee markers can be frequently changed to allow for an even distribution of wear.

Fairways

The fairway is the playing area between the tee and the hole. It is generally 40 to 65 yards wide and surrounded by rough consisting of tall natural grasses and weeds or unplanted natural terrain. The combination of the fairway and rough can reach 100 yards in side dimensions.

The playing area of each hole is designed in accordance with critical principles that are not apparent to most players. Fairway length determines par: up to 250 yards for a par-3 hole, up to 470 yards for a par-4 hole, and more than 470 yards for a par-5 hole from gold tees. Fairway width can vary greatly.

Narrow fairways require greater expertise; wider fairways favor less talented golfers. Landing areas, where most golf shots should fall, are planned at predetermined distances from the tee. Where the surrounding area is wooded, the fairway should be wider. Rough areas need to be carefully planned

FIGURE 2.1 A TYPICAL HOLE

17

The Game and Its
Facilities

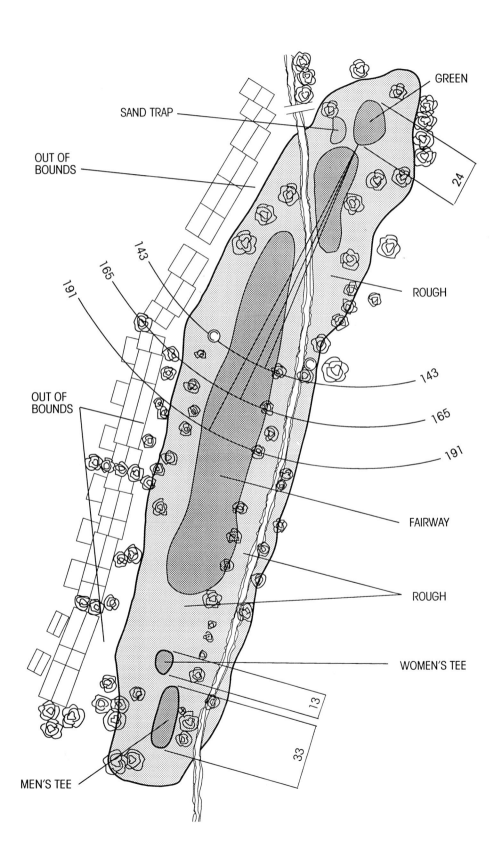

because they result in increased playing time. They can, however, materially reduce the costs of course construction if they are interspersed and extended between planned landing areas that are planted with turf, as in a traditional links design. The placing of hazards materially affects the difficulty or rating of the hole and the speed of play.

A path for golf cars may be an integral part of the fairway design. Such a path usually runs parallel to the length of the fairway, except where there are obstacles, and should be situated to follow the flow of the topography. Paved paths are necessary for courses that receive a great deal of play. The surface of the path may consist of gravel and rock, asphalt or concrete over a base, or dirt. A low-cost surface may produce initial savings, but could require excessive maintenance due to wear and tear, drainage problems, or exposure to the elements. Golf car paths are typically five to eight feet wide and approximately 20% to 40% longer than the course.

Greens

The putting area of a hole, or green, is carefully manicured to provide an even surface. Golfers need to study the terrain when putting because greens usually have a slight slope (for visibility and drainage) and grass has surface irregularities. Typical greens range in size from 3,000 to 5,000 square feet, but some may be larger; smaller greens are suitable for short approach shots; larger greens, which may range up to 1/2 acre in total area, are needed where the shape of the course is highly variable, course gets heavy play, or the typical approach is long or difficult. The size of the green should be adequate to allow for frequent changes in the location of the cup so that wear and tear on the surface is evenly distributed.

Greens vary not only in size and shape, but also in the variety of hazards that surround them. Most golfers as well as course designers and architects believe that the green should be contoured and visible from the location of the typical approach shot.

The construction of greens requires careful subsoil and drainage preparation. The site is prepared to a depth of eight to 24 inches with layers of gravel, sand, and soil mix over drainage tiles. The U.S. Golf Association establishes specifications for site preparation. In preparing a golf course appraisal, considerable attention should be given to the quality and condition of the greens because this is where the typical golfer spends a large percentage of his or her playing time. Greens are a key item in the rating of a golf facility.

Hazards

Sand bunkers, lakes, rough areas, and trees are typical golf course hazards. Hazards can be natural features or man-made features designed for a particular purpose. They make a course more challenging and some can provide other functions such as water storage, drainage, boundaries, and visual beauty. Their placement is important to the function of the game and can greatly influence the speed at which the typical golfer plays. Hazards add to the development and maintenance costs of a course.

Type of Holes

Individual hole styles fall into three broad categories: penal, strategic, and heroic.

Most golf holes have a strategic style, which means that golfers can se-

◄
A good sprinkler
system is a
necessity.

lect various means to reach the hole depending on their skills and the location of hazards. Strategic holes have wider fairways, but offer alternative routes such as a shot over a hazard that can reward the golfer with a lower score. To play penal holes all shots must go directly over hazards such as lakes, sand bunkers, or rough areas. Errant shots result in penalties, lost balls, and increased playing time. Courses with penal holes are designed for expert golfers and professional tournaments. Heroic golf holes represent a combination of strategic and penal styles. Their inclusion in a regulation course provides variety and challenges. Heroic holes are usually long holes over a water hazard that reward the successful golfer with a subpar score. Alternative routes (e.g., around the lake) are available for less skillful players and usually result in over-par scores.

Most golf courses provide a blend of styles with many strategic holes and a few that are heroic in nature.

Irrigation System

Climatic conditions dictate the size and complexity of golf course irrigation systems. Double-row systems with lines on each side of a fairway are popular, but in a wet climate, a less costly single-row layout may be adequate. Irrigation lines should be strategically placed based on the terrain and design of the course. Sprinkler heads are spaced so that the water coverage of the heads overlaps by as much as 100%. Automatic systems are preferred because of the savings in labor costs. A storage systems developed through a staged series of interconnected lakes can provide a continuous flow of water to the sprinkler system, which might not be possible with a typical combination of wells, pumps, and tanks.

Carefully controlled, cost-effective irrigation systems are a necessity in today's economic climate. Water will be an even more important economic issue in the future. Aside from the availability and cost of land, water for golf course irrigation will be the most decisive factor in the development of golf courses in the future. In areas where water quality and quantity are critical community issues, opposition to golf courses is common. One possible solution is more extensive use of treated effluent; this trend is expected to increase in the near future.

An appraiser valuing a golf course should be able to describe each elements of the irrigation system—i.e., linear feet of lines, number of sprinkler heads, number of valves, size and number of pumps and wells, and type and capacity of the storage system. The appraiser should also examine the system to understand the amount of accrued depreciation and estimate annual reserves for replacement.

THE CLUBHOUSE

The type of golf course and the objectives of the owners will dictate the size of the clubhouse and its facilities. A brief checklist is provided in Table 2.1. Functional considerations must be carefully analyzed before a commitment is made to design and build a clubhouse. Inappropriate clubhouses exist wherever there are golf courses, and many of these structures have incurable problems.

Because of high construction and operating costs, clubhouse architects must maximize the utility of each square foot of building area. Efficient management can then direct and control the workforce to minimize operating expenses.

Table 2.1 lists major rooms or functional areas that may be included in a clubhouse. Within each area a number of specialized activities may be conducted. A kitchen, for example, may include a chef's office, receiving area, dry storage area, meat and vegetable coolers, freezers, hot food preparation area, salad and dessert area, raw food preparation area, bakery, ice machines, dishwashing area, pot and pan washing area, serving stations, and garbage room.

More mistakes are probably made in clubhouse design and sizing than in any other aspect of golf course development. Often developers overdev-

TABLE 2.1 POTENTIAL CLUBHOUSE FACILITIES

1. Control fee collection	21. Service pantry
2. Administrative offices	22. Library
3. Golf shop	23. Nursery/children's room
4. Offices for golf staff	24. Meeting rooms
5. Storage room for pro shop	25. Patios/terraces
6. Changing room for pro shop	26. Bag storage/club repair
7. Lockers/restrooms/showers	27. Car storage
8. Steam rooms	28. Car maintenance
9. Saunas	29. Mechanical rooms
10. Whirlpools	30. Storage rooms
11. Card rooms	31. Employee lounge
12. Attendants' storage space	32. Maintenance offices
13. Exercise/fitness room	33. Linen/janitorial
14. Snack bars	34. Cold storage
15. Grill	35. Dry storage
16. Lounge	36. Service corridor/transport
17. Cocktail bars	37. Wine storage
18. Ancillary kitchen facilities	38. Loading dock
19. Dining rooms	39. Boiler room
20. Banquet room	40. Service pantry

elop the clubhouse with specialized facilities and choose an ornate design to make a social statement.

On a practical level, clubhouse architects should be able to analyze the specialized needs of the users of a facility through systematized research. Once the functions of the clubhouse are determined, it is wise to determine what percentage of the club membership or playing public will be engaged in each function and the frequency of use over a specified time period.

There are no hard-and-fast rules for determining clubhouse functions, but general concepts and probabilities can be cited. Obviously, all golf courses need a sheltered area for the collection of fees and the starting of play. The size of the pro shop or restaurant in a golf course is determined by studying competitive properties, the size and affluence of the membership, and the overall objectives of the management or owners. Overdevelopment of food and beverage facilities is a common problem in country clubs. In a resort complex, facilities such as restaurants, lounges, lockers and showers, kitchens, and offices can be provided by a hotel that is sited near the course(s).

The appraisal analysis typically involves *three* primary revenue-producing departments: pro shop sales, food and beverage sales, and car rentals. With few exceptions, the performance of the clubhouse as a functional unit of the golf course or country club is reflected in the income and expenses generated by these three departments. The financial viability of a clubhouse can be evaluated with careful cost accounting and analysis of the net gains or losses of individual departments.

In the application of the cost approach, economic data on clubhouse operations are needed to identify appropriate categories and amounts of depreciation and external obsolescence. These data are also needed in the sales comparison approach to adjust for differences in clubhouses of sale properties and the subject property. Such comparisons depend on relative measures of productivity, which may be based on pro shop sales per member or per round, food and beverage sales per square foot or per round, and car rentals per member or per round.

It is prudent to undersize a clubhouse if there is any question about its ultimate service requirements. Designing a clubhouse for expansion over its projected life cycle is extremely difficult, but this is preferable to building a facility that is too large or elaborate. Figure 2.2 shows various size requirements for clubhouses. This illustration was provided by golf course architect, Joseph S. Finger.

OTHER IMPROVEMENTS AND FACILITIES

A golf course and clubhouse cannot exist without a substantial number of ancillary land improvements and buildings. At a bare minimum, a course must have golf car storage space, which is frequently found on the lower or basement level of the clubhouse, and a maintenance building for the storage of equipment and supplies such as fertilizer. Additional structures may include a repair shop, a guard shack, rest stations, and pump houses. Regulation courses typically have up to 8,000 square feet of enclosed storage area, usually in a prefabricated metal structure.

Other recreational facilities associated with country clubs, exclusive real estate subdivisions, and resorts include tennis courts and swimming pools. These activities may be housed in separate clubhouse facilities with dressing rooms, a snack bar, offices, restrooms and lounges, and perhaps a fitness facility. Specialized appraisal textbooks should be consulted in valuing sports

FIGURE 2.2 THE GROWTH OF A CLUBHOUSE

22
Golf Courses and
Country Clubs

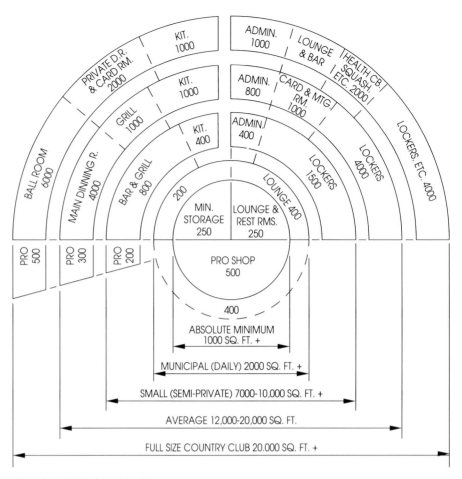

Source. Joseph S. Finger & Associates, Inc.

facilities that generate significant revenue or operating expenses for a golf course.[1]

Site improvements on a golf course include golf car paths, parking lots, driving ranges, service and entry drives, landscaping, and outdoor lighting. A driving range is a desirable aspect of any golf course and can be a significant profit center. Actually, a driving range is only one of the practice facilities found at a typical course; a putting green and chipping area are also common. A driving range should be located near to the clubhouse, have sufficient length (250 to 300 yards) and width to accommodate many golfers at one time, and have a designated space for golf instruction.

FURNITURE, FIXTURES, AND EQUIPMENT

In any analysis or valuation of a golf course, real property aspects of the project are emphasized. However, every golf facility includes a significant investment in furniture, fixtures, and equipment (FF&E), especially course maintenance equipment. A complex facility may have miscellaneous furniture in the lobby, office, and dining areas; office and kitchen equipment; pro shop furnishings; and maintenance tools and equipment.

1. One such text is *Fitness, Racquet Sports, and Spa Projects: A Guide to Appraisal, Market Analysis, Development, and Financing* by Arthur E. Gimmy, MAI, and Brian B. Woodworth (Chicago: American Institute of Real Estate Appraisers, 1989).

Golf cars are among the personal property included in the FF&E category. They can represent a large capital investment, but many clubs lease golf cars and other major items to reduce the amount of equity needed to develop and operate the course.

The total cost of FF&E can range from 3% to 9% of total assets. The market tends to indicate that the return on FF&E will be higher than the return required for real property. Moreover, furniture, fixtures, and equipment have a much shorter average life expectancy, typically five to ten years for individual items.

An appraisal should include an itemized inventory and estimate of depreciated value for the FF&E. This subject is discussed in relation to the valuation approaches in Chapters 7 through 10. A sample equipment inventory for a new course is shown in the appendix.

USES OF A GOLF FACILITY RATING FORM

To facilitate a golf course appraisal, a consistent format should be applied to the comparison of rental and sales data, green fees, and other golf course characteristics.

Golf course managers can use the golf course rating data to study the competition and identify the special benefits and unique aspects of a particular golf course facility. Rating data can assist in the preparation of a capital improvement program, help to identify deficiencies, and provide a reference for future market research.

The golf course rating form shown in Figure 2.3 illustrates the minimum information that would be gathered in analyzing competitive golf courses.

SPECIAL ENVIRONMENTAL CONSIDERATIONS

Proposed golf courses must satisfy planning and zoning requirements and meet environmental challenges. Environmental impact studies are required in most jurisdictions. Organized opposition to golf courses usually relates to the use of pesticides and fertilizers; the loss of open space, farmland, or wildlife habitat; and the inappropriate use of water.

Some of these problems can be alleviated with good management. For example, the seepage of pesticides and fertilizers can be reduced through controlled application. Water use can be managed more effectively with computer-controlled irrigation systems and the substitution of drought-tolerant plantings. Objections relating to the loss of agricultural land and employment are difficult to contest, but may be countered by promoting the beneficial aspects of a golf course such as employment opportunities, enhanced property and sales taxes, and higher real estate values. In drought-prone areas of the country, the water issue can be most important. A golf course cannot exist without proper irrigation. As mentioned earlier, increased use of treated effluent from waste water facilities is the contemporary solution to this problem. Thus, future golf course locations will be influenced by proximity to these plants. For golf courses in residential communities, onsite package plants can be used to reclaim domestic waste water for use on the golf course.

No investment in a prospective golf development should be made without first obtaining the services of professional consultants who can provide advice on environmental problems as well as planning and financial considerations.

FIGURE 2.3 GOLF COURSE RATING DATA

Name: _____

Address: _____

No. of holes: _____ Acres: _____ Length: _____

Par/course rating: _____ Zoning: _____ Age: _____

Annual rounds played: This year (est.) _____ Last year: _____

USGA slope rating _____

Description of buildings:

Type	Sq. Ft.	Condition/Design
_____	_____	_____
_____	_____	_____
_____	_____	_____

Type of irrigation: _____

List of Amenities: (please check)

Practice green	_____	Driving range	_____
Chipping green	_____	Practice sand trap(s)	_____
Lockers	_____	Bag storage	_____
Restaurant	_____	Snack bar	_____
Bar/lounge	_____	Golf cars	_____
Rain shelters	_____	Restrooms (on course)	_____
Drinking water (on course)		Snack bar (on course)	_____
		Tennis courts	_____
Swimming pool	_____		

Other (list items) _____

Course Rating: Use 1 to 5 points for each:

excellent = 5; good = 4; average = 3; fair = 2; poor = 1

Greens/fairways	_____	Clubhouse/pro shop	_____
Tees/range/hazards	_____	Trees/scenic beauty	_____
Layout/design	_____	Practice facilities	_____
Food/bev. facilities	_____	Other amenities	_____
Social atmosphere	_____	Course image	_____
Total points	_____		

Note: A score over 45 is excellent; 35–44 points is good; 25–34 points is average; 15–24 points is fair; and 14 points & under is poor.

Course Prices:

9-hole weekday $_____ 9-hole weekend $_____ 18-hole weekday $_____
18-hole weekend $_____ Golf car/9-hole $_____ 18-hole $_____
Special rates—Senior $_____ Junior $_____ Twilight $_____

Financial: Gross revenue $_____ Net income $_____
Sale price $_____ Date _____ OAR _____
TRM _____ GRM _____ PPR _____ GFM _____ Other _____

Date of rating: _____

Name of analyst: _____

Person contacted: _____ Telephone _____

CHAPTER THREE

THE PLAYER

 To project the demand for a golf course, it is necessary to analyze the recreational activities of certain segments of the population in a market area. Before this analysis is undertaken, however, the analyst should examine the behavior and attitudes of golf consumers. The National Golf Foundation (NGF) has produced two studies of the behavior and attitudes of golfers and two studies of non-golfers, including former golfers.[1] *Golf Consumer Profile*, 1987 and 1989 editions, and *Non-Golf Profile*, 1987 and 1989 editions, were based on a national sampling of golfers conducted by Market Facts, Inc. Selected data and findings from these studies are presented in this chapter. The serious student of golf is encouraged to obtain these original documents.

WHY PEOPLE PLAY GOLF

Golfers have many reasons for playing the game, but the primary ones relate to recreational enjoyment (first), being with one's friends (second), and relaxation (third).

Golf is generally considered nonstrenuous, but the sport can provide excellent exercise depending on the mode of transportation around the course. Walking a sloping or hilly course can be quite strenuous. On the other hand, if golf cars are used to maximum degree—e.g., driven off paths to the ball—the energy required to play a round is minimal. As a motive for playing, exercise ranks fourth. The rankings for eleven responses are shown in Table 3.1.

The analyst who wants a deeper understanding of the sport would be interested to know that seniors (79%), and females (66%) are more inclined to golf for exercise and depend on this activity to provide it. These and other gender differences can be emphasized in a marketing program for a golf course.

Statistics reveal many attitudes that contradict the public's image of golfers. Image, business reasons, and making contacts may rank low in reasons for playing golf because of many golfers' poor performance and high scores. The low ranking for business reasons may also be affected by the small percentage of individuals who are in a position to use golf as a business tool. Tax law changes relative to deductions for entertainment have had a negative impact on this aspect of the game.

The healthy aspects of the sport are the dominant reasons for playing golf and account for most of the responses. Golf can be played with little chance of injury, so its popularity will likely continue to increase as the population ages.

Phillip Gray has identified eight benefits which attract golfers to the game. They are: escaping pressures, social contact, escaping family, business de-

1. *"Golf Participation in the United States"* (Jupiter, Fla.: National Golf Foundation, July 1989).

TABLE 3.1

Ranking	Reasons for Currently Playing Golf	Percent of Respondents*
1	Recreational enjoyment	78
2	Because friends play	63
3	For relaxation	59
4	For the exercise	56
5	To get outdoors	54
6	For the challenge of the game	42
7	Relatives play	35
8	For the competition	27
9	Like the image of the game	16
10	To meet people/make contacts	15
11	For business reasons	14

* Percentages do not add to 100% due to multiple responses.
Source: Tables 3.1, 3.3, 3.4, 3.5, and 3.6 are reproduced from *Golf Consumer Profile, 1989 Edition* (Jupiter, Fla.: National Golf Foundation, 1989.)

velopment, exercise/physical fitness, social recognition/independence, meeting new people, and security. Gray's study concluded that "There is no relationship between benefits received by golfers and their social-economic standings; there are relationships between benefits received and frequency of play, skill levels, type of golf courses played most often and the golfer's 'psychographic' profile."[2]

WHY PEOPLE DON'T PLAY GOLF

About three-quarters of the population have never played golf. These individuals have many reasons for not participating in the game. Many of these reasons are economic in nature. In general, the possibility of adding this diverse group to the market is quite limited. Potential barriers to golf participation are set forth in Table 3.2.

A similar pattern of responses is found among former golfers, but to a lesser degree. Conflict with other recreational activities is the most important reason, followed by the three cost factors—equipment, green fees, and lessons—and hostile attitudes toward beginners. These figures suggest that,

TABLE 3.2

Ranking	Reasons for Not Playing Golf	Percent of Respondents*
1	Have other hobbies/play other sports	70
2	Cost of equipment too expensive	66
3	Green fees are too expensive	62
4	Cost of lessons/learning too expensive	54
5	Golf is not interesting	47
6	Golf takes too much time	45
7	Conflict with family responsibilities	45
8	Golfers don't like beginners on course	43
9	I don't fit image of golfer	41
10	Friends/family don't play	39
11	Golf does not provide enough exercise	23
12	Golf is too difficult/complicated to learn	18
13	No golf course nearby	17

2. Philip Gray, *"A Benefit Segmentation Study of Golfers,"* thesis.

* Percentages do not sum to 100% due to multiple responses.
Source: *The Non-Golfer Profile, 1989 Edition* (Jupiter, Fla.: National Golf Foundation, 1989.)

in certain segments of the population, financial inducements and making beginners feel more welcome could increase the size of the potential market.

TYPES OF GOLFERS

Like golf courses, golfers can be categorized in many ways. They were briefly identified in Chapter 1 by demographic factors: age groupings, household income, and occupation. (More complete data on demographics will be provided in Chapter 4.) The National Golf Foundation has identified golfers by attitude and divided them into five distinct segments: competitors, healthy sociables, outdoor relaxers, noncompetitors, and frustrated golfers.[3] The study, which was mentioned earlier, resulted in 16 psychographic labels identifying types of golfers. The NGF categories are not mutually exclusive, but they are useful to market researchers and those developing golf products. Some of the foundation's findings are summarized below.

Healthy sociables constitute the most active golfer group. Whereas the average golfer plays 22 rounds per year, the healthy sociable plays 47 rounds and has a better-than-average score of 91. Most have played golf for more than 10 years, are likely to be over 50 and retired. These golfers are the heaviest spenders on golf equipment, take more golf trips than any other segment of the population, read instruction articles, use golf cars, and have more time to enjoy the game.

The second most active group of golfers are referred to as competitors. They are usually male, play an average of 31 rounds per year, have the highest skill level with an average score of 88, and practice the game more often than other golfers. They are large spenders on golf equipment, are younger than most golfing groups, and tend to be better educated.

The last three behavioral groups—i.e., outdoor relaxers, noncompetitors, and frustrated golfers—play fewer rounds than the typical golfer, but represent many types of individuals commonly associated with golf.

Outdoor relaxers play an average of 17 rounds per year, are more likely to be female and older, and are less likely to use golf cars. These individuals rarely practice, spend less on golf equipment, and have an average score of approximately 95.

The typical frustrated golfer plays approximately 14 rounds per year and has an average score of about 97. This person is more likely to be young, with an average age of 35, and male. He spends less than the average amount on golf equipment and is better educated. The frustrated golfer segment of the market represents one fourth of all golfers; these individuals are frustrated when they play, mad when they play poorly, and miserable when they don't score well.

The last group of golfers are noncompetitors who, like outdoor relaxers, are passive in nature. These individuals play only about nine rounds per year, have an average score of approximately 32 over par, spend little on golf, and are more likely to be female and slightly younger than most golfers. People in this group usually do not care too much about their scores. They are happy when they hit the ball well and are the most likely individuals to quit the game. They make a good target market for campaigns to increase the number of golfers.

With a specialized market analysis an appraiser can identify the distribution of individuals who fall into these behavioral categories in a defined trade area. This information can be extremely useful in developing and marketing a proposed facility.

3. National Golf Foundation, *Golf Consumer Profile/Volume II* (Chicago: Market Facts, Inc., 1989)

► Most golfers play for
exercise and
recreation.

PLAYING CHARACTERISTICS

The performance of the typical golfer is of considerable interest to course
designers and managers. The scoring ability of players affects the number
of potential rounds and the desired difficulty of a planned course. Surpris-
ingly, the typical golfer finishes 18 holes on a regulation course at about 25
strokes over par. Men average 23 strokes over par and women average 12
strokes higher. A breakdown for various categories of golfers is shown in
Figure 3.1.

Additional data on playing characteristics have been compiled for hitting
distance (with driver and five-iron), golf ball trajectory, and warm-up and
practice. Hitting distance is important because it influences the placement
of tees and landing areas. The average male golfer drives a ball 199 yards
off the tee, while the average female hits the ball 131 yards. Using a five-
iron, men achieve an average of 137 yards and women drive slightly under
100 yards.

Distance becomes less important to scoring if the golfer is inaccurate.
Average golf scores are high partially because of the general flight pattern
of the ball. Nearly 80% of golfers hook, draw, fade, or slice the ball. The
groups with the shortest average driving distance (i.e., women and seniors)
hit the straightest. About 26% of women and 31% of seniors generally hit
the ball straight.

The poor quality of play exhibited by many golfers is probably due to a
lack of practice. Sporadic players, defined as those who play seven or fewer

FIGURE 3.1 AVERAGE STROKES OVER PAR

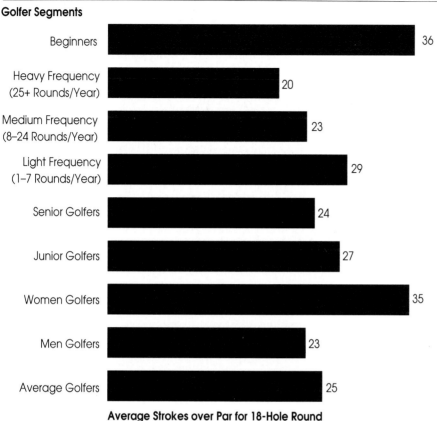

Golfer Segments

Segment	Strokes over par
Beginners	36
Heavy Frequency (25+ Rounds/Year)	20
Medium Frequency (8–24 Rounds/Year)	23
Light Frequency (1–7 Rounds/Year)	29
Senior Golfers	24
Junior Golfers	27
Women Golfers	35
Men Golfers	23
Average Golfers	25

Average Strokes over Par for 18-Hole Round

Source: National Golf Foundation

rounds per year, make up about 50% of all golfers. Most practice only a few times a year or not at all. Limitations on the time available for golf and the availability of convenient practice facilities appear to be the main reasons golfers do not practice more.

Speed of Play

The biggest playing problem facing golf course management is slow play. Slow play results in fewer rounds and reduced revenues for a golf course. According to the NGF's 1991 Consumer Profile, golfers average about three hours and 50 minutes to play 18 holes on a regulation course. The best golfers, those who score from zero to nine strokes over par, average three hours and thirty minutes. The poorest golfers, those who score 50 or more strokes over par, average about four hours. Thus, there is only a 13% difference in playing time between the two groups (i.e., 30 minutes divided by 230 minutes). Other findings from the survey follow.

- The average time needed to play a round of golf ranged from under three hours to over six hours.
- 25% of golfers said their slowest round in the last year took five hours or more.
- 15% of golfers said their slowest round in the last year took six hours or more.[4]

Given these statistics, there is room for improvement. For a typical course

4. Unpublished data obtained from Gordon Benson, PhD, of the National Golf Foundation.

on which 40,000 rounds are played, reducing the average playing time by 15 minutes could increase the number of rounds played by 2,500 rounds.[5]

The problems of slow play and crowding are related. About 25% of golfers say crowded courses are a reason they do not play more often. If management can speed up play by emphasizing golfing skills and enforcing rules, however, the extra time would probably be used to sell more rounds. Because there are more golfers than available facilities, the problem of overcrowding would persist.

The present situation may not be in the best interest of management. Some golfers state that they are planning to play less because they are bothered by slow play and overcrowding. If these golfers are among the better and faster players, the problem could get worse because the poorer players, who take longer, would then account for a larger portion of the rounds.

Management may also find that any programs or policies they institute to increase the speed of play may be unpopular with the majority of golfers. It is well established that the game of golf is played for relaxation and enjoyment. Many golfers expect to take about four hours to play a round and will resent management's attempts to make them move faster. Promoting the benefits of earlier starting times could help alleviate overcrowding.

Making the use of golf cars mandatory may speed up play at some courses. However, there is no clear evidence that golf cars can speed up the play of unskilled golfers and most players would likely resent such a requirement.

GOLFING EXPENDITURES

The 1986 NGF golf survey indicated that the average golfer spent $368 per year on the game. By 1988 that amount had increased to $551. The average amount spent per round was $22, but ranged as high as $26.20 per round for those in the highest income bracket. Table 3.3 shows that variations in the frequency of play do not significantly affect the amount spent per round; age and income factors are more likely to influence golfers' expenditures.

In addition to greens fees, golf expenditures include fees for golf car rental or caddies, use of driving range, and lessons as well as the cost of food and tips. This category of spending totaled $4.2 billion in 1988. Out of every dollar spent on golf, approximately $0.35 was spent on greens fees or their equivalent; $0.24 was spent on golf cars or caddies; $0.17 on food; $0.12 on lessons; and $0.06 each on driving range fees and tips. Table 3.4 provides a breakdown of golf-related expenditures.

Golfers also spend a great deal of money on clothing and equipment. Mean figures for expenditures can be misleading because many golfers spend nothing on certain categories of equipment in any one year. Nevertheless, this information can be useful in measuring the economic impact of golf and in projecting pro shop sales. Table 3.5 shows average expenditures for golfers who have spent money on various categories of clothing or equipment. These figures are used to derive a national figure based on the total number of golfers in the United States.

GOLF INSTRUCTION

5. A decrease in the average playing time from 4 hours to 3.75 hours represents a difference of 6.25%, which indicates 2,500 additional rounds (.0625 × 40,000 rounds).

As mentioned earlier, golf instruction represents one of the smallest expenditure categories related to playing golf. Given the difficulty of the game, one would expect that more money would be spent by golf consumers on individual and group lessons. Although more than 50% of golfers are dissatisfied with their golf game, 51.6% of all golfers surveyed report that they

TABLE 3.3 TOTAL ANNUAL GOLFER EXPENDITURES

Demographic Group	Average Amount Spent Per Year	Average Amount Spent Per Round
All golfers	$551	$22.00
Gender		
Male	$561	$22.37
Female	$518	$19.97
Age		
Under 20	$287	$18.32
20–39	$491	$22.62
40–59	$724	$23.48
60 and over	$639	$18.84
Income		
Under $20,000	$381	$18.39
$20,000–$49,000	$484	$21.25
$50,000-$74,000	$619	$24.82
$75,000 and up	$1,188	$26.20
Region		
Northeast	$509	$24.09
North Central	$390	$19.46
South	$764	$23.44
West	$582	$21.72
Playing frequency (rounds per year)		
Low (1–7)	$311	$22.02
Average (8–24)	$576	$22.14
High (25+)	$1,041	$21.14

Source: *Golf Consumer Profile, 1989 Edition.*

TABLE 3.4 EXPENDITURES RELATED TO PLAYING GOLF

Expense Item	Percent of Golfers Purchasing	Average Annual Expenditure*	National Market
Golf cars/caddies	55.3	$131.30	$1.7 billion
Driving range	51.6	$33.03	$398 million
Lessons	11.1	$63.99	$165 million
Food	78.9	$92.74	$1.7 billion
Tips	27.7	$34.92	$226 million

*Calculated only for those golfers reporting expenditures
Source: *Golf Consumer Profile, 1989 Edition.*

TABLE 3.5 GOLFER EQUIPMENT EXPENDITURES

Equipment Item	Percent of Golfers Purchasing	Average Annual Expenditure	National Market (millions)
Balls	80.5	$31.48	$593
Clubs	31.4	$95.38	$700
Bags	17.5	$50.63	$207
Shoes	35.9	$50.04	$420
Gloves	54.2	$18.75	$237
Clothes	39.8	$78.04	$726
Other equipment	52.8	$17.10	$211
Total market			$3,094

Source: *Golf Consumer Profile, 1989 Edition.*

never had a golf lesson. An additional 19.3% said their most recent golf lesson was more than five years ago. Only about 10% of all golfers indicated they had a lesson within the past year—i.e., 8.7% of male golfers and 16.4% of female golfers.

Annual income is a key indicator of expenditures on golf instruction. The higher the income, the greater the proportion of golfers who have taken lessons recently. In 1988, only 18% of golfers earning less than $20,000 had taken a lesson within the past three years, compared to 34.8% of golfers in the $75,000 annual income bracket. Figure 3.2 shows the proportions of various types of golfers who have had a lesson within the previous year.

Approximately two out of three lessons are received on an individual basis and about one-third are taught in groups. About three-quarters of all lessons are given at a golf facility, where 57% are given on the course and 43% on the driving range. The remaining lessons were given in a school setting at a stand-alone driving range or on a practice putting green.

About 85% of those receiving lessons in the past year felt that the lessons were somewhat or very helpful in correcting their weaknesses, but less than half felt that their scores were lowered as a result of their most recent golf lesson. Based upon all these factors, it appears that greater revenue could be generated by golf facilities from golf instruction and education. Most golfers who do not take lessons are infrequent players who are not serious about the game and feel that lessons are too expensive. Lack of convenience or distance from home do not appear to be significant factors. The entire field of instruction has been underperforming and a well-managed, publicized program could be a catalyst for greater golf participation and club revenues.

FIGURE 3.2 PROPORTIONS OF GOLFER GROUPS TAKING A LESSON IN PAST YEAR

Percentage

All Golfers	10.4
Low Frequency	3.1
Average Frequency	10.7
High Frequency	19.3
20 Years	15.7
30-39 Years	8.8
40-59 Years	12.1
60+ Years	9.5
Male	8.7
Female	16.4

Source: National Golf Foundation

◀

More golf instruction could promote greater participation and club revenues.

Golf Travel

Resort-oriented golf courses derive a substantial portion of their revenue from vacationing golfers. Golf-related travel and lodging was reported by Sports, Inc. to be approximately $7.8 billion in 1988.

For analyzing this segment of the market, a golf trip is defined as any trip, regardless of its purpose (business, vacation, or other), that originates from a consumer's home, necessitates at least one overnight stay, and involves playing golf at least once. Playing golf at a seasonal residence is counted as one trip and includes all golf played while at that residence.

About one-third of all players take golf trips each year. It is difficult to generalize about the characteristics of these travelers, but it is safe to say that wealthier golfers and those who play most frequently are the two groups most likely to take trips. Table 3.6 breaks down golf travelers by age, income, and frequency of play.

In recent years the golf vacation market has grown significantly. The 1986 *Golf Consumer Profile* revealed that the average golf traveler took 2.2 golf trips that totaled 12.4 days and included 5.9 days playing golf. By 1988 this figure had increased to 3.1 golf trips, averaging 13.7 days with 6.7 days of golf.

There is a huge potential market for golf among players who travel either for business or pleasure. The significant market for well-located resort properties has been apparent for a number of years. Many resort facilities have been constructed recently in Sunbelt states and in the Caribbean and Hawaiian islands. Analysts involved in determining the financial feasibility of such projects should carefully study the market data provided by the NGF.

TABLE 3.6 PROPORTIONS OF GOLFER GROUPS WHO TOOK TRIPS

Demographic Group	Percentage of Group
Age	
Under 20	24.6
20–39	32.3
40–59	42.3
60 and over	36.5
Income	
Under $20,000	21.6
$20,000-$49,999	33.9
$50,000-$74,999	41.3
$75,000 and up	51.3
Play frequency (rounds per year)	
Low (1–7)	20.5
Average (8–24)	41.9
High (25+)	56.7

Source: *Golf Consumer Profile, 1989 Edition.*

CONCLUSION

The material in this chapter has shed light on the identity and characteristics of golf consumers. This information will serve as a backdrop for the analysis of supply and demand presented in the following chapter.

CHAPTER FOUR

SUPPLY AND DEMAND

 The supply of golf courses and the degree of participation in the game varies by geographic region. Therefore, national statistics do not accurately indicate local conditions. A complete state-by-state analysis is beyond the scope of the book but major regional differences and trends as well as sources of information can be identified.

The primary source of supply data for golf courses in the United States is *Golf Facilities in the United States* published by the National Golf Foundation. This annual publication contains data on national, regional, state, and metropolitan areas. The best source of demand data is another annual publication of the NGF, *Golf Participation in the United States*. Both of these reports are available for purchase. Within individual states or metropolitan areas, supply data may be obtained from golf associations and institutional research departments.

Golf statistics compiled by the National Golf Foundation are presented throughout this chapter. These data are derived from a national sample of the population and are subject to error. The foundation is continually improving its research efforts to provide the most accurate information available, but appraisers are cautioned to use these statistics in combination with actual field research and other primary data.

A basic knowledge of golf terminology is needed to understand the statistics and data presented.

Golf capacity utilization is the number of rounds played on a course divided by the desired number of rounds. A private course may prefer to express capacity utilization as the actual number of club members divided by the maximum number of members desired.

Golf participation rate is the percentage of the total population in a defined area, age five and older, who have played golf at least once within a calendar year.

Golf frequency rate is the average number of rounds played per year by a defined segment of the golfing population.

Golf accessibility rate is the total population of a defined area compared to the number of golf holes; the rate is expressed in terms of the number of persons for each 18 holes.

SUPPLY

At the end of 1990 there were 13,951 golf courses in the United States. The characteristics of these courses—i.e., type, length, and operational category—were shown in Table 1.3.

Market studies of golf projects are based on the number of golf rounds that can be supported by a given trade area. To estimate the supply of golf rounds an appraiser studies the inventory of courses, determines the desired number of rounds per facility, and converts these data into the total number of desired rounds available for play in the trade area.

Desired rounds vary from course to course and are a function of a number of variables, including budgets, management policy, course conditions, and past operating history. The owner of a daily fee course may want to achieve 47,000 rounds per year, while the recreation and parks department of a city may prefer to operate at a level of 69,000 annual rounds. Obviously, average performance figures for individual courses are insufficient. Each course in the trade area being studied must be analyzed to develop a true picture of the supply of golf rounds.

The number of *desired* rounds will typically be greater than the number of actual rounds even in an undersupplied market because playing conditions vary. Changes in weather, family pressures, time restrictions, and a lack of information as to course availability can affect the number of rounds played. Nevertheless, the golf market is usually tight, so the number of actual rounds played is probably close to the number desired in many places. This is demonstrated by national statistics, which show an estimated 506 million rounds played in 1990 with a total supply of 201,213 holes, resulting in an average number of rounds played per 18 holes of 45,265 in 1990.

The term *capacity utilization* used in the golf business is equivalent to the *occupancy factor* of a lodging facility, as used in real estate analysis. The capacity utilization for a public course is the number of actual rounds divided by the number of desired rounds; the capacity utilization for a private course is typically shown as the number of actual members divided by the number of desired members. Thus a public course with 55,000 desired rounds per year and 47,000 rounds actually played would have a capacity utilization rate of 85%. Similarly, a private club would be rated at 93% capacity utilization if it had 560 members and a limit of 600 members. It should be noted that some public courses achieve a capacity utilization over 100% by letting more golfers play than is recommended for proper maintenance of the facilities.

The supply of golf holes and the capacity utilization of courses vary greatly on a regional and state-by-state basis.

DISTRIBUTION OF FACILITIES

Golf facilities of all types and lengths are unevenly distributed throughout the United States. Statistics by course type and length on a regional, state-by-state, or metropolitan area basis are available from the National Golf Foundation. For the analyst, the most meaningful statistic is the golf accessibility rate because it expresses supply in terms of the total population of an area.

Golf accessibility by state is illustrated in Table 4.1. The table shows the number of state residents for each 18 holes available and includes separate totals for private and public facilities. High figures suggest an underserved market, while low figures may indicate that a state has an adequate supply or an oversupply. The analyst must recognize, however, that the supply within a state or metropolitan area may appear to be adequate, but it can still be unevenly or disproportionately distributed. Thus some local trade areas can be overserved or underserved.

For all golf facilities the range of golf accessibility by state (excluding Alaska) extends from a low of 40,801 persons per 18 holes in California to a high of 11,245 persons in South Dakota. For private courses South Dakota

TABLE 4.1 GOLF ACCESSIBILITY BY STATE

State and Region*	1990 Population	Total			Public			Private		
		Holes	Pop. Per 18-Holes	Rank	Holes	Pop. Per 18-Holes	Rank	Holes	Pop. Per 18-Holes	Rank
Connecticut	3,271,920	2,556	23,042	28	1,296	45,443	36	1,260	46,742	14
Maine	1,216,930	1,449	15,117	9	1,152	19,015	4	297	73,753	41
Massachusetts	5,923,910	4,761	22,397	25	2,907	36,681	29	1,854	57,514	22
New Hampshire	1,127,660	1,260	16,109	15	1,071	18,952	3	189	107,396	47
Rhode Island	1,005,580	702	25,784	40	378	47,885	37	324	55,866	20
Vermont	568,850	810	12,641	4	648	15,801	1	162	63,206	31
New England	13,114,850	11,538	20,460		7,452	31,678		4,086	57,775	
New Jersey	7,864,320	4,167	33,971	46	1,998	70,850	46	2,169	65,264	33
New York	18,001,250	11,214	28,894	44	7,137	45,400	35	4,077	79,476	43
Pennsylvania	12,022,360	9,702	22,305	24	6,021	35,941	28	3,681	58,789	24
Middle Atlantic	37,887,930	25,083	27,189		15,156	44,998		9,927	68,700	
Illinois	11,646,490	8,694	24,113	31	5,616	37,328	30	3,078	68,108	35
Indiana	5,586,230	5,697	17,650	18	4,086	24,609	14	1,611	62,416	28
Michigan	9,269,600	11,016	15,146	10	8,586	19,433	6	2,430	68,664	36
Ohio	10,860,990	10,674	18,315	20	7,560	25,860	17	3,114	62,780	30
Wisconsin	4,860,740	5,661	15,455	11	4,428	19,759	8	1,233	70,960	39
E. North Central	42,224,050	41,742	18,208		30,276	25,103		11,466	66,286	
Iowa	2,835,070	4,059	12,572	3	2,223	22,956	12	1,836	27,795	2
Kansas	2,525,430	2,862	15,883	14	1,350	33,672	25	1,512	30,065	4
Minnesota	4,345,200	5,013	15,602	12	3,762	20,790	10	1,251	62,521	29
Missouri	5,187,410	3,636	25,680	39	2,061	45,305	34	1,575	59,285	26
Nebraska	1,605,900	1,971	14,666	8	1,134	25,490	16	837	34,535	6
North Dakota	678,200	1,053	11,593	2	720	16,955	2	333	36,659	8
South Dakota	714,040	1,143	11,245	1	657	19,563	7	486	26,446	1
W. North Central	17,891,250	19,737	16,317		11,907	27,046		7,830	41,129	
Delaware	661,640	468	25,448	37	126	94,520	48	342	34,823	7
District of Columbia	622,400	153	73,224	50	99	113,164	49	54	207,467	50
Florida	13,037,110	16,614	14,125	7	8,694	26,992	20	7,920	29,630	3
Georgia	6,539,930	4,779	24,633	33	2,196	53,606	40	2,583	45,574	13
Maryland	4,682,130	2,313	36,437	47	909	92,715	47	1,404	60,027	27
North Carolina	6,664,540	7,659	15,663	13	4,419	27,147	21	3,240	37,025	9
South Carolina	3,559,090	5,067	12,643	5	3,069	20,874	11	1,998	32,064	5
Virginia	6,130,500	3,978	27,740	43	1,953	56,502	41	2,025	54,493	19
West Virginia	1,896,260	1,485	22,985	27	1,017	33,562	24	468	72,933	40
South Atlantic	43,793,600	42,516	18,541		22,482	35,063		20,034	39,347	
Alabama	4,152,940	3,051	24,501	32	1,197	62,450	43	1,854	40,320	11
Kentucky	3,767,210	3,060	22,160	23	1,737	39,038	31	1,323	51,255	16
Mississippi	2,661,050	1,935	24,754	34	756	63,358	44	1,179	40,627	12
Tennessee	4,962,950	3,402	26,259	42	1,818	49,138	38	1584	56,397	21
E. South Central	15,544,150	11,448	24,440		5,508	50,798		5,940	47,103	
Arkansas	2,431,450	2,016	21,709	22	837	52,289	39	1,179	37,121	10
Louisiana	4,549,010	2,070	39,557	48	684	119,711	50	1,386	59,078	25
Oklahoma	3,335,920	2,322	25,860	41	1,431	41,961	33	891	67,392	34
Texas	17,682,340	10,809	29,446	45	5,301	60,042	42	5,508	57,785	23
W. South Central	27,998,720	17,217	29,272		8,253	61,066		8,964	56,222	
Arizona	3,671,400	3,744	17,651	19	2,466	26,799	18	1,278	51,710	17
Colorado	3,448,890	2,736	22,690	26	1,782	34,837	26	954	65,073	32
Idaho	1,016,200	1,116	16,390	17	882	20,739	9	234	78,169	42
Montana	814,190	909	16,123	16	603	24,304	13	306	47,894	15
Nevada	1,104,720	855	23,257	29	738	26,944	19	117	169,957	49
New Mexico	1,565,790	1,116	25,255	36	711	39,640	32	405	69,591	37
Utah	1,774,190	1,287	24,814	35	990	32,258	23	297	107,527	48
Wyoming	494,500	639	13,930	6	468	19,019	5	171	52,053	18
Mountain	13,889,880	12,402	20,159		8,640	28,937		3,762	66,459	
Alaska	568,390	99	103,344	51	72	142,098	51	27	378,927	51
California	29,336,220	12,942	40,801	49	7,857	67,208	45	5,085	103,845	46
Hawaii	1,130,360	1,089	18,684	21	801	25,401	15	288	70,648	38
Oregon	2,774,060	2,097	23,812	30	1,566	31,886	22	531	94,036	45
Washington	4,704,140	3,303	25,636	38	2,358	35,909	27	945	89,603	44
Pacific	38,513,170	19,530	35,496		12,654	54,784		6,876	100,820	
United States	250,857,600	201,213	22,441		122,328	36,913		78,885	57,241	

*See page 152 for a map of the regions used in this analysis.

Source: National Golf Foundation, *Golf Facilities in the United States, 1991 Edition* (Jupiter, Fla.: National Golf Foundation, 1991.)

is again ranked first in accessibility and Nevada is ranked last; for public courses Vermont is first and Louisiana is last. In a general discussion of golf course supply, population relative to all types of courses is meaningful; an appraiser or analyst, however, would analyze the population relative to the supply of the particular type of course under consideration.

Golf course accessibility statistics show that there is a great variation in supply. While the figures may indicate the general situation, a norm for golf statistics may never be known. It can be discerned that many states are underserved even though capacity utilization rates as low as 85% can be found in the Sunbelt. Weather can make a 100% difference in the number of playing days in a Frostbelt state as compared to a Sunbelt location. Thus, 11,245 persons per 18 holes in South Dakota can amount to about the same golf accessibility as 27,754 persons per 18 holes in Mississippi.

When examined on a metropolitan area basis, golf accessibility statistics become more refined and meaningful. NGF presents data for 320 metropolitan statistical areas (MSAs) broken down by estimated population, the total number of golf holes, and the number of public and private holes. To provide a relative indicator or ranking of the supply of golf facilities, figures are shown by the resident population per hole, or *PPH*.

The national PPH average for 1990 is 1,452 residents for each golf hole within metropolitan areas. Public golf holes average 2,503 PPH and private golf holes average 3,462 PPH. There can be a wide variance in the accessibility of different types of facilities in an area. For example, Roanoke, Virginia, ranks 178th with a lower-than-average PPH of 1,321. However, it has a higher-than-average PPH of 3,138 for public golf holes (ranking 230th), but a much lower-than-average PPH of 2,282 for private golf courses (ranking 62nd).

PPH statistics must be used very carefully. The figures are based on the total population, not the golfer population. Furthermore, certain Sunbelt locations attract many tourists and seasonal residents. Population data for year-round residents will not reflect the true demand for golf in these areas.

In general there is a serious shortage of golf facilities in the United States, as evidenced by the imbalance between the rapid increase in the number of golfers and the slow increase in the supply of facilities. Recent increases in supply have done little to alleviate the situation.

DISTRIBUTION OF GOLFERS

Golfers are everywhere and they are not deterred by climatic conditions. Some of the highest participation rates are found in Frostbelt states with the shortest playing seasons and some of the lowest rates are in Sunbelt states.

Participation rates range from a low of 4.0% of the population in the District of Columbia to a high of 16.6% in Minnesota. The national average is 12.2%.

To a great extent differences in participation can be explained by differences in golf accessibility. Comparing the supply data in Table 4.1 to the golf participation rankings in Table 4.2 indicates a fairly close correlation between the availability of courses and the golf participation rate. For example, of the top 15 states in terms of participation rate, 11 were ranked among the top 20 in terms of golf accessibility. Conversely, of the lowest 15 states in terms of participation, 11 were also ranked in the lowest 20 in terms of golf accessibility.

Many other factors influence the participation rate such as degree of affluence (measured by household income, education, and occupation) and

TABLE 4.2 GOLF PARTICIPATION BY STATE, 1990

State	Golf Participation Rate (Percentage)	Total Golfers
Alabama	7.9	264,000
Arkansas	5.6	109,000
Arizona	13.7	416,000
California	11.8	2,842,000
Colorado	14.5	409,000
Connecticut	12.8	354,000
District of Columbia	4.0	23,000
Delaware	9.3	52,000
Florida	12.3	1,374,000
Georgia	9.5	510,000
Iowa	17.4	394,000
Idaho	17.0	130,000
Illinois	16.0	1,530,000
Indiana	13.8	639,000
Kansas	13.8	288,000
Kentucky	11.1	345,000
Louisiana	5.6	201,000
Massachusetts	14.3	720,000
Maryland	10.0	392,000
Maine	10.8	109,000
Michigan	16.9	1,273,000
Minnesota	21.2	727,000
Missouri	11.7	499,000
Mississippi	5.3	110,000
Montana	13.6	88,000
North Carolina	11.0	609,000
North Dakota	19.3	99,000
Nebraska	15.0	194,000
New Hampshire	9.5	90,000
New Jersey	11.0	730,000
New Mexico	13.6	171,000
Nevada	13.0	118,000
New York	10.9	1,643,000
Ohio	15.3	1,375,000
Oklahoma	9.6	257,000
Oregon	12.9	291,000
Pennsylvania	10.8	1,071,000
Rhode Island	10.9	93,000
South Carolina	10.0	290,000
South Dakota	13.0	77,000
Tennessee	8.5	358,000
Texas	10.5	1,497,000
Utah	21.0	267,000
Virginia	9.4	469,000
Vermont	11.6	55,000
Washington	13.4	510,000
Wisconsin	19.3	769,000
West Virginia	8.8	135,000
Wyoming	17.4	67,000

Source: National Golf Foundation

age (measured by the percentage of the population aged 50 or more). As an example, the states with the lowest participation rates also tend to be the least affluent.

States that have emphasized the development of public courses tend to have the highest participation rates. Many of these states are located in the North Central region of the United States. Seven out of the 14 states with the highest golf accessibility rates (Iowa, Kansas, Michigan, Minnesota, North Dakota, South Dakota, and Wisconsin), are also among the 14 states with the highest participation rates. Moreover, seven of the 14 states with the lowest golf accessibility rates (Georgia, Louisiana, Mississippi, Oklahoma, Tennessee, Texas, and Virginia), are not only among the least affluent states in the United States, but are also among the lowest 14 in terms of golf participation.

The state that comes closest to exhibiting the average performance for the entire nation is Colorado. Its participation rate is 12.3% and it is ranked right in the middle in terms of golf accessibility. States with favorable demographics that are significantly underserved with golf facilities include California, Maryland, Missouri, New Jersey, New York, Oregon, Rhode Island, Tennessee, Texas, Virginia, and Washington.

Detailed data on participation are not reported on a state-by-state basis, but they are reported by region. Table 4.3 shows participation rates broken down by gender, age, household income, education, and occupation.

Gender

One in five men play golf while only one in 18 women take part in the game. The Northeast and South fall below the mean, while the North Central region, as expected, has the highest participation rates. The West is close to the national norm for both sexes. Participation rates in recent years have been growing in the West, but not as fast as they have in the South.

Age

The highest participation rate in all regions is found among young adult golfers in the 18–29 age bracket. The rate varies, however, from one in eight in the South to one in five in the North Central region. Participation rates decline as the age of the population increases; at the same time the difference in participation rates between regions decreases. Thus, for the 18–29 age group there is a 40% difference between the high and low participation rates, but for the 65 and over group the difference is only about 25%. Similarly, there is only a negligible difference of 200 basis points between the participation rates of senior golfers in the North Central and Western regions. This is probably due to the health consciousness and outdoor orientation of westerners who play even though western states are ranked among the lowest in golf accessibility.

The median age of all golfers was 35.5 in 1990 and has been dropping. Median age varies only slightly from region to region with the lowest age of 35.1 in the North Central, followed by 35.6 in the West, 35.7 in the Northeast, and 35.8 in the South.

Household Income

In every region in the United States, golf participation increases as household income increases. Rates of participation vary greatly by region, however. For individuals with household incomes of $10,000 to $19,999, the rates

TABLE 4.3 PARTICIPATION RATES
CATEGORIES OF GOLFERS BY DEMOGRAPHICS AND REGION, 1990

Demographic Categories	USA	Northeast	North Central	Southern	Western
Total population	12.3	10.4	14.7	8.8	11.6
Gender:					
Male	19.4	17.4	22.3	14.7	17.9
Female	5.6	4.0	7.5	3.3	5.4
Age:					
5–12 years	2.5	3.2	4.8	2.5	3.4
13–17 years	10.2	8.8	13.8	7.4	10.0
18–29 years	16.5	15.2	20.9	12.9	16.6
30–39 years	16.3	13.5	19.4	10.9	15.3
40–49 years	13.9	11.8	17.8	10.3	13.0
50–59 years	12.2	10.6	15.2	9.2	11.9
60–64 years	11.8	9.9	14.7	8.6	11.2
65+ years	8.5	7.1	9.2	6.7	9.0
Household income:					
Under $10,000	3.6	2.9	5.6	2.6	4.2
$10,000-$19,999	6.5	5.7	8.3	4.6	7.5
$20,000-$29,999	10.5	8.9	12.9	7.8	9.6
$30,000-$39,999	11.8	10.5	15.6	9.6	12.2
$40,000-$49,999	15.5	12.9	19.3	12.3	14.1
$50,000-$74,999	17.7	14.5	21.8	14.4	15.2
$75,000+	22.2	17.1	27.0	19.6	20.0
Education:					
Secondary school	4.5	4.1	5.2	3.0	4.2
High school graduate	9.2	7.8	12.2	6.2	8.9
Some college	13.0	11.4	16.1	9.4	11.1
College graduate	18.9	16.0	22.4	15.1	16.9
Occupation:					
Blue collar	9.8	8.5	12.4	6.3	9.9
Clerical/sales	14.6	12.2	17.3	10.6	13.5
Prof./mgmt./admin.	18.3	15.1	22.7	14.4	15.9
Other	9.2	7.5	11.2	6.3	9.1

Source: National Golf Foundation

vary from a low of 7.4% in the South to 13.8% in the North Central region. Participation is highest in the income bracket over $75,000 per year. For example, one out of every 3.7 persons in this group in the North Central area is a participant.

Education and Occupation

Golf participation increases with the level of education. Similarly, as occupational status and pay increase, the rate of golf participation also grows.

Trends

Golf participation rates increased more than 9% per year between 1985 and 1990. By age groupings, the greatest increase was for individuals between 18 and 29 years old. By gender, male participation increased from 3.3% to 5.6%. By region, the West saw the greatest numerical increase, growing from a participation rate of 7.9% in 1985 to a rate of 13.4% in 1990. In the South, the rate increased from 5.3% in 1985 to 9.4% in 1990.

Conclusion

Participation rates are useful in developing market feasibility studies. When used with a variety of demographic data, they can be a valuable tool in estimating the probable number of golfers within a defined area. Separate estimates can be made by applying participation rates to age, household income, education, and occupation categories.

ROUNDS PLAYED

The number of rounds played is a function of the participation and frequency rates applied to the population of a defined trade area. Potential demand in terms of number of rounds can be calculated as

$$
\boxed{\text{Population}} \times \left(\text{Participation}\right) = \boxed{\text{Golfers}} \times \left(\begin{array}{c}\text{Frequency}\\\text{Rate}\end{array}\right) = \boxed{\text{Rounds}}
$$

The most direct evidence of potential golf course activity is indicated by statistics on the number of rounds played by specialized population groups.

A participant who plays only once a year has a negligible impact on the market. Studies conducted by the NGF have resulted in golf frequency rates for a wide variety of demographic and psychographic categories which can be of great assistance to the market analyst. Demographic information for defined trade areas is available from computer-generated sources such as MAX and CACI.

It is useful to analyze the number of rounds played by golfer frequency groupings. An overview of nationwide performance shows that in 1990 occasional golfers (i.e., those who play one to seven rounds per year) comprised 55% of all golfers, but only accounted for 9.5% of all rounds played. At the other end of the scale, frequent golfers (i.e., those who play 25 or more rounds per year) comprised only 20.1% of all golfers, but accounted for close to 72% of all rounds played. When the group that plays eight to 24 rounds per year is included with frequent golfers, one can see that approximately 45% of all golfers (the core group) accounted for more than 90% of all rounds played. Table 4.4 presents data for 1990.

TABLE 4.4 GOLFERS AND ROUNDS PLAYED, 1990

Frequency Category	Golfers (Millions)	Percent of All Golfers	Average Rounds/ Golfer	Rounds Played (Millions)	Percent of All Rounds
Occasional (1–7 rounds per year)	15.705	55.3	3.1	48	9.5
Average (8–24 rounds per year)	6.984	24.6	13.8	96	19.0
High/frequent (25+ rounds per year)	5.711	20.1	63.4	362	71.5
Totals	28.400	100.0	17.8	506	100.0

Source: National Golf Foundation

In recent years there has been continued growth in the number of golfers, but a slight decrease in the frequency of play. The mean number of rounds per golfer declined from 20.2 in 1986 to 19.4 in 1987, then increased to 20.8 in 1988 and again declined to 19.2 in 1989 and 17.8 in 1990. Most of the drop was attributed to the frequent golfer group whose average number of rounds went from 65.9 in 1988 to 63.4 in 1990. The occasional golfer group's average number of rounds also declined from 4.5 in 1989 to 3.1 in 1990.

Demographic categories help the analyst estimate the number of potential rounds available from a defined trade area more precisely. The data in Table 4.5 shows play frequency, or average annual rounds played, by gender, age, income, geographic region, education, and occupation.

Six major findings can be drawn.

1. Male golfers play 37% more rounds per year than female golfers.

2. Frequency of play increases dramatically with age—e.g., golfers over 60 play about three times as many rounds per year on the average as golfers 18–39 years old.

3. Frequency of play varies moderately with income, but in an unexpected way. Persons in the $10,000-$19,999 income bracket have the largest number of annual rounds, followed by those in the highest income bracket, and then by those in the fifth highest bracket.

TABLE 4.5 ROUNDS PER GOLFER PLAYED IN THE UNITED STATES, 1990

Population	0	10	20	30	40	50	Total Rounds (in millions)	Percent of All Rounds
Total			17.8				506	100.0
Male			19.0				413	81.6
Female		13.9					93	18.4
Age								
5–12 years		7.6					7	1.4
13–18 years		11.3					20	3.9
18–29 years		11.6					90	17.8
30–39 years		12.7					87	17.2
40–49 years			17.0				76	15.0
50–59 years			23.9				64	12.6
60–64 years				36.5			46	9.1
65 years and over					43.2		116	22.9
Household Income								
Less than $10,000		12.8					11	2.2
$10,000–$19,999			23.4				60	11.9
$20,000–$29,999			19.5				82	16.2
$30,000–$39,999			15.6				68	13.4
$40,000–$49,999			15.4				65	12.8
$50,000–$74,999			16.9				134	26.5
$75,000 and over			20.5				86	17.0
Geographic Location*								
New England			18.8				29	5.7
Middle Atlantic			15.9				67	13.2
East North Central			16.3				104	20.6
West North Central			18.0				46	9.1
South Atlantic			21.5				92	18.2
East South Central			19.9				27	5.3
West South Central			22.1				46	9.1
Mountain			15.9				29	5.7
Pacific			16.0				66	13.1
Education								
Non-high school grad			19.5				26	5.1
High school grad			18.8				131	25.9
Some college			18.3				149	29.4
College grad			16.8				200	39.5
Occupation								
Prof. mgmt./admin.			15.1				167	33.0
Clerical/sales			16.4				73	14.4
Blue collar			14.1				92	18.2
Other/retired				27.4			174	34.4

*See page 152 for a map of the regions used in this analysis.
Source: National Golf Foundation

4. Sharp differences in frequency are exhibited on a geographic basis. Many Frostbelt regions such as New England, East North Central, and West North Central have equal or higher rates than Sunbelt states in the Mountain and Pacific regions.

5. Level of education has little bearing on the number of annual rounds played, but college graduates have the lowest frequency.

6. Occupation is not a significant determinant of annual rounds played but frequency increases when a golfer retires. Golf frequency for the 65+ age bracket is substantially higher than for any type of demographic category.

CHAPTER FIVE

MARKET AND FEASIBILITY ANALYSIS

 The previous chapter introduced the major characteristics of the golf market and sources of primary and secondary data available for analysis. This chapter addresses how such data are used to measure the market support for a specific golf facility.

Simply stated, a market analysis is performed to forecast the future demand that may reasonably be expected for a specific facility. The value of a golf facility is based largely on the expectation of future benefits, typically measured as future income, which in turn is based on demand. Because a market analysis serves as the foundation for any estimate of value, it is of critical importance and requires close attention. A value estimate is only as sound as the underlying market analysis.

Market analysis is a creative process. Every facility and every market is unique, so each market analysis must be tailored to fit the specific situation. However, the analytic process, as described in this chapter, is virtually identical for all facilities and markets (although it requires modification for certain assignments). This process serves as the basic structure for all market analyses. It is the application of this structure that requires creativity.

One cannot simply impose the model from one facility onto another. For example, demand for one facility may be based on local demand for golf (measured, say, in rounds per capita within a 10-mile radius); demand for another facility may be based on tourist demand (measured, perhaps, in rounds per lodging room night); a third market analysis may require examination of a combination of both these factors. Creativity is required to identify relevant variables, to determine how they can best be measured, and to interpret the results.

The market analysis process requires all the judgment and knowledge of the analyst. Forecasting demand requires familiarity with and knowledge of a large number of variables and their effect on demand. Many variables such as wind direction, sun, lighting, and local values are difficult or impractical to quantify. The effect of individual variables may be minor, but collectively they can have a significant impact. All significant variables must be identified and factored into the analyst's judgment process to project demand.

This chapter will address the theoretical framework of market analysis, which may be applied to existing or proposed facilities, different types of facilities, and different market environments. Practical examples are presented to illustrate market analysis in specific situations and to introduce specific data commonly used in market analyses and appraisal assignments.

FIGURE 5.1 MARKET ANALYSIS FLOWCHART

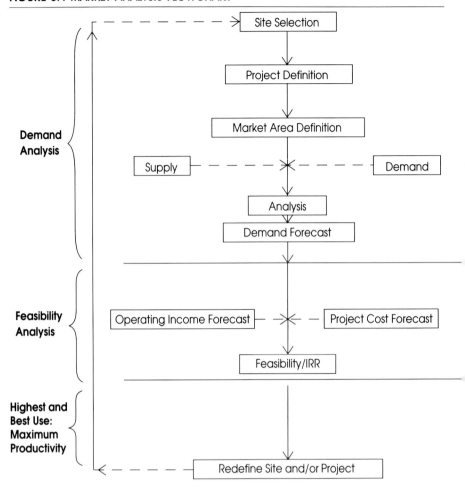

THE ANALYTIC PROCESS

Figure 5.1 is a flow chart depicting the market analysis process for a golf facility. This illustration will serve as the basic outline for this chapter. An overview of the entire market analysis process is presented below, followed by a detailed discussion of each step in the process.

There are three basic types of market analysis—demand analysis, feasibility analysis, and maximal productivity (highest and best use) analysis—which are defined by the functions they serve.

Demand Analysis

The objective of a demand analysis is to forecast the demand for a specific, defined facility.

Feasibility Analysis

A feasibility analysis pertains to a hypothetical facility—i.e., a proposed facility or the redefinition of an existing facility. A feasibility analysis begins with a demand analysis of the hypothetical facility. Once demand is determined, the internal rate of return (*IRR*) is measured by forecasting all operating cash flows (income and expenses) and all development costs. The resultant *IRR* is compared to alternative investment opportunities or to a benchmark or desired yield rate to determine the feasibility of the project.

Maximal Productivity (Highest and Best Use) Analysis

One aspect of highest and best use analysis, which is discussed in detail in the following chapter, is the examination of alternative uses of a property to determine which use yields the highest *IRR*—i.e., is maximally productive. (The focus here is on golf-related uses, although other uses that may yield higher *IRRs* should be investigated.) To identify the alternative use that is maximally productive, the site or project is redefined and demand and feasibility analyses are then performed on that alternative use. The process is repeated for all reasonable alternatives. The maximally productive alternative is the use with the highest *IRR*. (Although there may be virtually unlimited alternatives, the maximal productivity analysis is facilitated by computer modeling and other methods of triaging alternatives, which will be discussed in this and subsequent chapters.)

The following discussion of market analysis focuses on an existing facility. A nearly identical process is applied to a proposed facility, but an existing facility is typically more rigidly defined. Considerations specific to proposed facilities are noted as appropriate.

Note that in developing new facilities or changing existing ones, maximal productivity is typically realized when the design is market-driven. The early involvement in the development team of individuals experienced in the market analysis of golf facilities often helps identify market opportunities and avoid pitfalls. Their suggestions can then be incorporated into the design process. Too often a market feasibility analysis is one of the last development functions performed. After the plans have been drawn, the developer discovers that an alternative use or design concept would yield a higher *IRR*, which sometimes makes the difference between a feasible project and an infeasible project. Difficult decisions then must be made. It is very important to let the market dictate the design as the latter is easier to change than the former.

DEMAND ANALYSIS

Site Selection

Clearly site selection is most relevant in the early stages of development. However, the criteria applied in selecting a site are also applied in evaluating a predetermined or existing site, and the evaluation process is the same.

Chapter 2 examined many of the physical characteristics important to a golf course site: natural amenities; environmental conditions such as wind, sun, noise, air quality, and odors; topography; and characteristics affecting the ease of development, including soil conditions, water availability, and grading requirements. Beyond these factors, market conditions must also be assessed. The study of the supply and demand characteristics of a region often reveals market niches of unmet demand, which can direct the selection of a site. The location of competing facilities is critical because developers want to locate new golf courses in areas with little competition. Other site selection criteria are proximity to population centers with favorable demographic characteristics, and favorable neighborhood characteristics including proximity to complementary uses such as beaches, yacht clubs, harbors, ski hills, and open space.

Project Definition

For an existing facility, the project definition is simply a description of the property. Nevertheless, this early step in the process is critical because it establishes the direction of the market analysis. The objective of the analysis is to forecast demand, so the question to be answered is "Demand for what?"

The project definition must be inclusive and critical. It should incorporate the appraiser's full knowledge of the game of golf, its players, the characteristics of a golf facility, and the market. All variables that can affect demand positively or negatively must be described and critiqued.

The description of the project must extend to both tangible and intangible variables that may affect demand. A clear example of one intangible variable is price. To forecast the number of rounds played annually at a facility, one must define the price at which these rounds will be played, recognizing the relationship between price and demand. Other project characteristics that must be defined include type of facility (e.g., public, private, resort), condition, difficulty of play, ancillary amenities (e.g., conference facilities, clubhouse, pro shop, tennis courts), aesthetics, environmental conditions, and name recognition. The list is virtually endless. The analyst must succinctly identify the most significant variables and be aware of all others and their cumulative impact.

In the analysis of a proposed facility, the stage of the project and the scope of the assignment may limit the level of detail required in the project description. For example, in the earliest, conceptual stages of a project, simply determining if there is a demand for any type of golf course may be sufficient. This general determination calls for a substantially different level of descriptive detail than an appraisal of a fully designed facility that is being valued for construction financing. The appraisal of a planned facility for financing purposes would require a level of descriptive detail equivalent to or exceeding that required in the appraisal of an existing facility.

Market Area Definition

Once the project is defined, the market area, or market segment, may be defined. The market area is identified by delineating the geographic boundaries of the target population from which the project will draw its patrons.

The market area is defined in accordance with the characteristics of the subject facility. Ideally, the subject characteristics were developed based on the needs of a properly targeted market area. For example, the demand analysis for an exclusive, expensive private country club may target households within a 15-mile radius with incomes of more than $75,000 per year. An older course in fair condition with some adverse environmental condition may be targeted to appeal to households within five miles with incomes below $40,000, a market interested in economy and convenience.

The target market may be defined by a large number of parameters, including income level, golf skill, topographic barriers, local vacationers, age, and business/conference patrons. Multiple parameters may be employed. The only imperative is that the target market be compatible with the project description.

Some appraisers use a simple method of defining the market segment, by driving time to the facility. This method is valid if the project is compatible with the demographics of the target market so defined. A 1989 golf consumer survey by the National Golf Foundation ascertained the distance in driving time and miles that golfers travel from their homes to the course at which they most often play. The results are summarized in Table 5.1.

Based on this survey, the market area is often defined simply as the area within a 30-minute drive of the site. This 30-minute driving-time radius rep-

TABLE 5.1 DISTANCE TO MOST FREQUENTLY PLAYED COURSE

Time		Distance	
Minutes	Percentage of Respondents	Miles	Percentage of Respondents
Under 10	19	Under 2	12
10–14	20	3–5	26
15–19	19	6–9	15
20–24	17	10–14	18
25–29	5	15–19	11
Over 30	20	Over 20	18

Note: The average travel time was 20 minutes; the average distance traveled was 13 miles.
Source: *Golf Consumer Profile* (Jupiter, Fla: National Golf Foundation, 1989.)

resents the driving distance of 85% of all golfers. When this is transcribed into distance, an area with a 15-mile radius may be indicated and the population within this area is the defined market.

Forecasting Potential Demand

The next step in the demand analysis is forecasting the total potential demand for the subject's defined market area. Note that this demand forecast includes both the satisfied demand currently met by the subject and its competitors and unsatisfied demand.

Potential market demand must be measured for a specific time period. The value of a facility is based on its economic life. With proper maintenance, the life of a golf course can extend well beyond 50 years. Practically, a 10-year forecast is specified and quantified. Of course, projections become more tenuous in later years due to a variety of uncertainties. However, golf facilities have long economic lives, so one should also consider their potential beyond the 10-year projection. Although a longer-term forecast may not be quantified or detailed in an appraisal report, it is necessary to identify anticipated long-term demand.

Clearly, demand must be measured in relation to specific services. The analyst must forecast demand for all services and products offered by the subject facility. Demand for golf play may be divided into demand for club memberships, guest rounds, daily fee rounds, and conference/business rounds. The unit of measure typically applied to golf demand is rounds per year. In addition to golf play, demand for other products and services must be forecast, including golf car rental, driving range use, pro shop merchandise, and food and beverage service. This discussion will focus on forecasting the level of golf play; all other services may be forecast using the same methodology.

In current marketing practice, there are six methods by which demand may be forecast. Of these, three are appropriate to golf facilities: 1) statistical demand analysis, 2) direct survey of players' intentions, and 3) expert opinion. (The other three methods, which are generally inappropriate for golf facilities, are sales force composite opinions, test-market methods, and time-series analyses.) A great deal has been published on these six methods of demand forecasting, and the reader is referred to this body of literature to augment the basic information presented herein. The following discussion highlights the three forecasting methods appropriate to golf facilities, beginning with statistical demand analysis.

Statistical Demand Analysis

Statistical demand analysis is the forecasting method most commonly applied in real estate appraisal. It is also given strong consideration in other real estate and business endeavors. Many factors affect the demand for any golf facility. Statistical demand analysis attempts to identify the most important factors (e.g., population, income) and forecast demand based on how units of demand relate to these factors. Forecasting based on the projection of historic demand for comparable facilities or in comparable markets also falls within this methodology.

In statistical demand analysis, demand is expressed as an independent variable (Y) which may be explained as a function of a dependent variable (X). For example, demand may be directly related to the population within the subject's geographically defined market area. If one knows the number of rounds played per capita, demand may be forecast based on future population projections within the market.

The procedure begins by identifying those factors on which demand is most dependent. These are drawn from the definition of the market area, which in turn is derived from the project definition. Demand is commonly measured in relation to the age, income, skill level, or club membership patterns of the total population, or simply the total number of residents within a geographic market. Demand can also be related to the number of business managers and executives in the market area or the number of tourists visiting the area.

In forecasting demand for peripheral services the most common factor used to measure demand is the number of rounds of golf played. For example, food and beverage demand may be projected at $7.00 per round of golf based on sales activity at similar clubs. This factor is then applied to the projected number of rounds to forecast food and beverage demand.

The next step is to measure the relationship between the independent variable and the demand for golf. This is drawn from market-derived data, which may be either "primary" or "secondary" data.

Secondary Data. Secondary data typically pertain to macromarket characteristics (i.e., on the state or national level); primary data relate directly to the subject's specific micromarket. Secondary data include golf participation rates and frequency of play rates, from which demand per capita may be derived, as well as information on income levels, age, and geographic characteristics. These data were discussed in detail in Chapter 4.

Secondary data show the relationship between the dependent and independent variables such as rounds per capita. Secondary data are readily available and generally statistically valid, but they are generic in nature and may not accurately reflect the idiosyncrasies of the specific subject market. The analyst must be sensitive to this problem and make appropriate adjustments.

Primary Data. Primary data offer several advantages over secondary data. If properly acquired and analyzed, they yield more accurate and appropriate evidence of demand and its relationship to independent variables. Also, primary data may be tailored to meet the specific information requirements of the assignment and the characteristics of the market being investigated. Primary data typically must be acquired by the appraiser or by independent consultants, which may require considerable time, expense, and expertise. Nevertheless, certain primary data are required for all appraisals.

Primary data may relate to the same characteristics as secondary data, but the focus is on a smaller market. Primary data are more specific to the assignment requirements and may measure the ratio of rounds to private club members, hotel room nights, local residents, or other factors.

The past demand performance of the subject market, including the demand for the subject property itself, provides the most valuable type of primary data. These data can reveal ratios and relationships among independent variables within the local market. It is important that course and market capacity be carefully examined. Since the objective is to measure market potential, the demand experience of courses operating at capacity will not reflect unsatisfied potential demand. A thorough investigation of actual demand is required for both the demand forecast and competitive analysis, and for the ultimate forecast of the subject's demand. Indications of desired rounds as opposed to actual rounds may be obtained from the golf pro or manager of each competitive facility.

One excellent data source, especially for proposed facilities, is a different market area with characteristics similar to the subject market area. Data from another market developed through field research can be used as a test market from which demand may be measured. Consider a proposed course in a tourist area with no existing golf courses. A comparable tourist area with existing golf facilities can provide excellent data on tourist rounds per room night, which can then be applied to the subject's market. Again, one must determine the capacity of the facilities in this comparable market to satisfy the full potential demand.

Potential Demand Forecast. Once the required data are obtained, demand may be forecast with statistical demand analysis. The appraiser simply forecasts an independent variable, such as population, and applies the relationship between it and the dependent variable, such as rounds per capita, to project the future demand potential.

The forecast of the independent variable is frequently generated by secondary sources. Secondary data may be obtained from sources such as the Census Department's population projections. Regression analysis, tempered with appraisal judgment, is commonly used to generate forecasts of primary data for the subject market.

A simple example is presented in Table 5.2, Statistical Demand Analysis Projection. This is called a *projection* because it projects past relationships and acts as a tool in making the subsequent *forecast*.

The example indicates the importance of using both primary and secondary data. The ratio of rounds per capita and rounds per capita among individuals over 50 with incomes over $40,000 are greater in the subject market than national averages indicate. If this information is combined with an expanding population of individuals in this age and income group, the indicated demand potential would differ substantially from that suggested by the secondary data alone.

Demand is often projected based on the past demand performance of the subject market. When this method is applied, the number of rounds played annually is the dependent variable and the year is the independent variable. Historic performance is regressed to project future demand. (Data from years during which golf courses in the market were operating at capacity may not be used.)

The simple method of analysis described above produces a projection,

TABLE 5.2 STATISTICAL DEMAND ANALYSIS PROJECTION

	Rounds per Capita	×	Target Population	=	Potential Rounds
Secondary Data					
Demand by Location					
National	2.163		162,000		350,406
Local (state)	2.341		162,000		379,242
Demand by Age					
5–19	0.605		11,000		6,655
20–29	1.83		9,000		16,470
30–39	1.638		21,000		34,398
40–49	2.269		40,000		90,760
Over 50	3.848		81,000		311,688
Total			162,000		459,971
Demand by Income					
Under $10,000	0.538		5,000		2,690
$10,000-$20,000	1.174		11,000		12,914
$20,000-$30,000	1.811		20,000		36,220
$30,000-$40,000	2.592		58,000		150,336
Over $40,000	3.286		68,000		223,448
Total			162,000		425,608
Primary Data (15-mile radius)					
Total population	2.982		162,000		483,084
Over 50 years	3.989		81,000		323,109
Over $40,000	4.321		68,000		293,828

Conclusion
Range .... 350,000 to 485,000 rounds
Mean .... 420,000 rounds
Median .... 425,000 rounds
Indicated potential rounds .... 425,000 rounds

not a forecast. This distinction is necessary because of three problems associated with the statistical demand analysis method of forecasting.

1. The forecast of the dependent variable is only as good as the forecast of the independent variable. However, the independent variable can often be forecast with a relatively high degree of accuracy. Demographic and economic parameters may be quite reliable because forecasting techniques for these parameters are well developed and reasonable forecasts are readily available.
2. Many other independent variables can affect demand.
3. The relationship between the dependent and independent variables may not be known definitively (i.e., it may not be a constant ratio), and this relationship may change.

Recognizing these problems, the projections are used as benchmarks which direct the appraiser's judgment in developing the forecast. This illustrates the advantage of performing demand analysis in a number of ways, using both primary and secondary data and a variety of independent and dependent variables.

The analyst's judgment requires a thorough analysis and understanding of the market environment. Such analysis is essential to real estate appraisal and is repeatedly addressed in appraisal literature. In *The Appraisal of Real Estate*, the market environment is characterized by four types of forces: social, economic, governmental, and environmental.

1. Social forces which relate to the demographic characteristics of the population may profoundly affect the demand for facilities. For example, certain nationalities have a penchant for the game. Similarly, aging baby boomers, well-educated individuals, and upper-income professionals exert above-average demand. Other, less easily identifiable factors can indicate that certain communities will have more avid golfers than others.

2. Economic forces are analyzed to determine the economic base which supports a community and its potential demand for the game. Employment, wage levels, business trends, and the overall economic base of the region and the community are among the economic forces analyzed.

3. Governmental forces can profoundly affect the golf market. For example, many popular areas of the nation have taken a no-growth posture, which discourages golf course development.

4. Environmental forces include both natural and man-made forces. As previously mentioned, golf demand is particularly sensitive to natural forces such as snowfall, rain, wind, and topography. Man-made highways, airports, and real estate developments can also affect demand.

With a thorough understanding of the market environment and all the variables that affect demand, the appraiser can adjust the projection to forecast the potential demand for golf facilities in the subject market area based on statistical demand analysis.

Survey of Players' Intentions

Useful information regarding future demand in a specific market can be derived by interviewing players on their future intentions. This increasingly common method of estimating demand may be applied using questionnaires, direct personal interviews, or focus group studies.

These survey studies can be costly and time-consuming, but the results can serve as an excellent indication of demand. In addition, such studies often help identify significant market opportunities and may facilitate the design of proposed facilities or the operation, management, or reconfiguration of existing facilities.[1]

Because of the time and cost involved, formal survey studies are usually conducted only before major capital investments are made in proposed facilities. On the other hand, informal studies are an integral part of all appraisals. Extremely valuable information can be missed if the appraiser does not make a point of questioning every informed person. Useful information may be obtained from players, pros, managers, and employees of the subject and competing facilities as well as community leaders and other knowledgeable individuals.

In survey research, a consultant is retained to sample the target population through mailed questionnaires, telephone interviews, or one-on-one interviews. Of these methods, questionnaires often produce the best response rate because respondents can remain anonymous. Moreover, the results are easy to analyze and tabulate. Questionnaires can be distributed at golf courses, where the consultant can control the time and method of distribution. The survey must be tailored to the stage of project development and the information needed, which typically extends beyond the number of rounds the player may be expected to play on the course. The questions

1. Two texts on focus group techniques are Richard A. Krueger, *Focus Groups, A Practical Guide for Applied Research* (Sage Publishing, 1988) and David W. Stewart, *Focus Group, Theory and Practice* (Sage Publishing, 1990).

posed may relate to the player's socio-economic profile, golfing habits and preferences, and price sensitivity.

In formal focus group studies, comprehensive questions are put to groups of five to 20 golfers or potential golfers. The purpose of a focus group study is to test the acceptance of the subject, its physical design and service package, the proposed location, the relative merits and drawbacks of competing facilities, consumer price sensitivity, and expected demand patterns. The questioning sessions usually last a few hours and are open-ended and non-judgmental. There are no correct answers to the questions, which are designed only to gather information.

Expert Opinion

Another method of forecasting involves tapping the opinions of well-informed persons such as golf pros, managers, and owners. The usefulness of these opinions depends on the individual's qualifications, availability, and reliability. The opinions offered by individuals who are not affected by the subject property are typically more reliable, but these persons may be less qualified. The information provided by experts cannot serve as the sole, or even primary, basis of the forecast, but it can be quite valuable in analyzing the results of other methods. Therefore, expert opinions should always be sought.

Demand Forecast Summary

Based on the projections generated and the data acquired, the appraiser can forecast the potential demand in the subject's market area. The reliability of this forecast depends on factors such as the quality and quantity of data available, the number of different methods used to project demand and their correlation, the time period studied, and the skill and experience of the appraiser.

The degree of certainty associated with the forecast should be indicated. Typically, a single demand figure (e.g., number of rounds) is forecast for each year and represents the most likely demand. This figure may be established with varying degrees of certainty. For example, the first year demand figure derived from an established market in which no changes in market conditions are expected can be forecast with greater confidence than the potential demand in a new market with no existing golf facilities. Usually the certainty of the forecast is discussed in general terms. Some appraisers quantify the probability of occurrence, but this technique is not yet common in this industry. Likewise, estimates of varying future levels of demand can be generated, but this exercise is rarely performed.

Supply Analysis

After a demand forecast for the subject's market area is prepared, the analysis turns to the investigation of supply, specifically existing and future competitors within the market. Clearly the subject's share of the potential demand is directly related to the competitive environment. Because the golf market is specialized and shallow, it is vital that all competing facilities be specifically identified. A thorough analysis of the competition is not vital for forecasting the demand for the subject, but is necessary for highest and best use analysis. Such an analysis can also help an owner or developer design or modify a facility and its services to satisfy market preferences and tap unsatisfied demand.

Defining the subject and its market area sets the parameters for the identification of competitors. Competitors must be loosely defined to include any facility that may compete for the potential demand in the subject's target market area. By this definition, competitors need not be within the subject's target market area, either physically or in terms of facility or service characteristics; they may be peripheral to it. For example, the target market may be defined geographically as the area within a 15-mile radius of the subject. A facility located 20 miles away may also have a 15-mile target market. Obviously this second facility is a competitor in that overlapping area. This situation is presented graphically in Figure 5.2.

FIGURE 5.2 OVERLAPPING COMPETITION

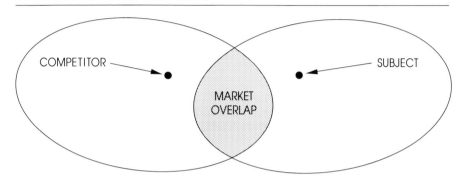

Overlapping competition extends beyond geographically defined competitors and markets; it also applies to the facilities and services offered. Direct competition exists among similarly defined facilities and markets; indirect competition exists among facilities and markets defined as dissimilar, but overlapping. Both types of competitors must be identified.

Identifying competitors for golf facilities is usually quite easy. The owner, pro, and manager of the subject usually know the competition well, so they are an excellent source of preliminary information. To ensure that all competitors are identified, similar individuals at competing facilities should be consulted as well as players at these facilities, local tourist bureaus and chambers of commerces, and the National Golf Foundation. These sources plus the local planning department can also provide information pertinent to proposed facilities.

Once competitors are identified, the appraiser should visit each facility and gather the required information. Interviews of varying depth can be conducted with owners, pros, managers, and players. The objective is to develop a clear and complete profile of each facility. The more directly the facility competes with the subject, the greater the quantity and quality of data required. A sample data checklist is provided in Figure 2.3; the data required can be modified somewhat depending on the nature of the assignment. In addition to eliciting specific information, the appraiser should ask open-ended questions such as "What would make this course more popular?" to ferret out as much information as possible.

Competitive Analysis

If there is no competition within the subject's market area, and the subject offers the only tangible and intangible product for which market demand was forecast, the subject will capture the entire demand up to its capacity and the analysis is complete. (For a proposed project, however, the appraiser must forecast the absorption rate.)

Of course, it is rarely this simple because typically competition does exist. Usually the appraiser must perform a competitive analysis to determine the relative ability of the subject and its competitors to capture the potential demand of the target market. The objective of this analysis is to determine the subject's market share. A method commonly used in competitive analysis is demonstrated in the following example. This method can serve as an excellent starting point for the comparison of many facilities.

Consider the situation depicted in Figure 5.2 in which a competing facility is located 20 miles from the subject and the facilities' 15-mile markets overlap. Assume that the facilities are otherwise identical. Commercially available demographic data services can provide demographic information on the overlapping area as well as information on the subject's target market. With generated demand data measured in rounds per capita and population statistics on the overlapping area, one can project, and then forecast, the total potential rounds generated. If the two facilities are equally desirable, it may be reasonably concluded that the competitor will capture 50% of this demand. The competitor's captured demand is then deducted from the total potential demand in the subject's target market to yield the total demand that the subject will capture. The process is illustrated in Figure 5.3.

FIGURE 5.3 GEOGRAPHIC MARKET SHARE ANALYSIS

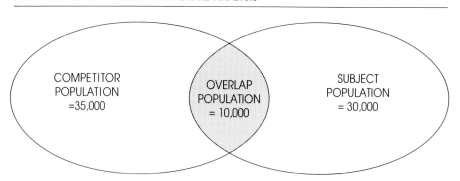

If the rounds per capita equal 2.0, and the subject will capture 50% of the overlapping market, then:

Subject demand $= (30,000 \times 2.0) - (10,000 \times 2.0 \times 50\%) = 50,000$ rounds

This example is a simplification of the process; rarely are the two facilities equal. However, the method shown can serve as a starting point for analysis. Some parameters used in the analysis may be quantified. If, for example, one facility were an expensive private country club, and the other a public daily fee course, data on the type of course played by golfers of various income levels could be applied to the income levels of the overlapping population to refine the market share analysis.

Typically the number of variables is large and their relationship to demand is often unquantifiable, so a more subjective adjustment of the relative market shares of competing facilities is required. In performing competitive analysis, the appraiser identifies all pertinent variables, focusing on those that have the greatest impact on the facilities' ability to their capture market share. These variables may include location, price, level of difficulty, aesthetics, associated amenities (e.g., pro shop, clubhouse, tennis courts, pool), condition, name recognition, and status. Clearly, the variables pertinent to each comparison are unique. The weighting process described in Figure 5.3

can help the analyst judge the capabilities of the subject as compared to its competitors.

Demand Forecast

The demand forecast is complete once the potential demand for the subject's market area is forecast and its competitive share of this market is estimated. Figure 5.4 presents an example of how demand is estimated using three separate techniques.

FIGURE 5.4 FORECAST OF ANNUAL ROUNDS FOR PROPOSED RESORT/COUNTRY CLUB

Information: R/CC is a proposed golf community/resort project situated in a seasonal resort city where the economy is supported primarily by tourism (i.e., ski sports in the winter and sightseeing/shopping in the summer). There is a resident population of 28,000 persons within a 30-mile radius; the level of annual visitors has reached 350,000 room nights. The overall outlook for increased tourism is good. There are no golf courses in the community. The nearest facility is 25 miles away and reached by a two-lane road.

Research: Market analysts studied the operating history of all golf courses within a radius of 100 miles. In a highly comparable city 85 miles away, there are three golf courses. Their patronage is derived from tourists and residents (full and part-time). The number of room nights in this market is 925,000 and annual golf rounds total 105,000.

Estimates: Three separate measures of golf demand can be made for R/CC.

A. *By comparison to comparable city.* In the comparable market, 40 rounds are played per 1,000 room nights of lodging and 650 rounds per 1,000 residents. Applied to the 350,000 room nights and 28,000 persons in the subject market, this resulted in an estimated demand of 32,200 rounds calculated as follows:
1. 350,000 room nights × 40/1,000 = 14,000 rounds
2. 28,000 residents × 650/1,000 = 18,200 rounds
3. Total 32,200 rounds

B. *By direct comparison with area courses.* The primary country club in the comparable city had realized 40,000 rounds, but this club is superior to the proposed subject. Two facilities in communities similar in size to the subject trade area have achieved 35,000 and 30,000 rounds. Their season is eight to nine months per year. The course situated 25 miles away does only 18,000 rounds, but it is poorly maintained and has a season of only six months. The golf season at R/CC is estimated at eight months. Overall, these facilities, none of which are competitive, indicate approximately 30,000 to 35,000 rounds for the subject.

C. *By NGF participation rates.* The subject resident population was divided into household income brackets to determine the number of golfers. Average rounds per golfer by income was determined from NGF data. The estimated number of potential rounds for the subject calculated with this methodology is 38,806.

Household Income	Population	Percent Golfers*	No. of Golfers	Rounds per Golfer[†]	Rounds
$0–10,000	10,136	3.6	365	12.8	4,672
$10–20,000	7,912	6.5	514	23.4	12,028
$20–30,000	4,256	10.5	447	19.5	8,716
$30–40,000	2,897	11.8	342	15.6	5,335
$40–50,000	1,195	15.5	185	15.4	2,849
$50–75,000	1,062	17.7	188	16.9	3,177
$75,000+	448	22.2	99	20.5	2,029
	27,906		2,140		38,806

*Derived from data in Table 4.3.
[†]Derived from data in Table 4.5.

Conclusion: The number of annual rounds estimated for the proposed golf course is 32,500, with a potential range of 30,000 to 39,000. Greatest emphasis was placed on local comparables.

Demand must be forecast for each service and product offered by the subject—e.g., driving range, golf car rental, food and beverage, merchandise sales—in addition to golf rounds. These forecasts may be made using the techniques discussed, but in practice the demand for many services is forecast in terms of their relationship to the demand for rounds of golf—e.g., golf car rental revenue per round. (For further discussion, see Chapter 8.)

Comparables Forecasting

Comparable forecasting is a method of forecasting demand based on the experience of comparable facilities. For example, if an identical facility in an identical market realized 50,000 rounds, so would the subject. If the facilities are dissimilar, adjustments for such dissimilarities are made.

This method is, in fact, a portion of the methodology described in this chapter. The identical facility provides the basis for determining the demand ratio (e.g., in rounds per capita). When this ratio is applied to the subject market's population, a quantified adjustment is made for the population difference of the markets. Adherence to the methodology outlined in this chapter simply ensures consideration of all relevant factors. The omission of an important factor is the most common error in market analyses, and may have significant consequences.

FEASIBILITY ANALYSIS

The type of feasibility analysis addressed here pertains to the financial feasibility of a project. While the feasibility of a project may be analyzed in legal, environmental, or physical terms, this discussion is limited to financial feasibility analysis. Financial feasibility analysis may, however, be influenced by legal, environmental, or physical factors.

The objective of a feasibility analysis is to forecast the internal rate of return on and of invested capital for a proposed project. If this *IRR* meets or exceeds the rate required by the investor, then the project may be deemed feasible. Feasibility is of vital importance to developers, lenders, and potential investors in any proposed project. The flowchart shown as Figure 5.5 graphically depicts the structure of this analysis.

FIGURE 5.5 FEASIBILITY ANALYSIS FLOWCHART

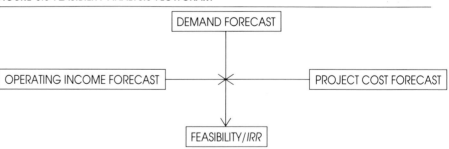

In determining a project's *IRR*, the primary task is to identify and quantify all cash receipts and expenditures attributable to the proposed project. This analysis begins with the forecast of demand, which serves as the basis for forecasting the net operating income the project will generate. (This process will be discussed in detail in Chapter 8 in relation to the income approach to value.) Simply, a property's net operating income is the difference between all operating revenues and all expenses, excluding the capital costs of development.

Conceptually, the forecast extends over the entire economic life of the project. Practically, the projection period used extends one to two years beyond the time at which the property reaches a stabilized income pattern. This usually covers a period three to 10 years from commencement of construction, when the projection period typically begins. A sale of the property is assumed in the stabilized year, based on direct capitalization of the following year's expected net operating income. The net proceeds of this sale, which exclude sale costs, represent the last cash flow item realized in the projection period. Even if the project is not sold, this item represents the expected value of the cash flows over succeeding years. This pro forma analysis is typically made on an annual basis, although monthly or quarterly forecasts are appropriate when the total projection period is relatively short such as one to three years.

The next step of a feasibility analysis is to forecast all the capital costs of the project. (This process is addressed in detail in Chapter 7 in relation to the cost approach.) Capital costs include the costs of raw land, land development, hard construction, landscaping, equipment and fixtures, all consulting fees and permits, interest reserves, marketing prior to opening, management systems development, start-up personnel expense, and contingencies. These must be forecast as of the time period in which they are expended.

An example of such a cash flow analysis is summarized in Table 5.3, Feasibility Analysis for Proposed 18-Hole Golf Course. In this example, an option to purchase the land is executed at the beginning of Year 1. Construction begins immediately and extends through the beginning of Year 2. Year 2 is a period of course cultivation, growth, and grooming as well as premarketing and installation of management systems and personnel. The course opens for play at the beginning of Year 3. Following a three-year absorption period, stabilized operations are reached in Year 6. Some upgrading is required prior to sale of the facility. Year 6 cash flows include the receipts of an assumed sale at the end of the year, based on the expected net operating income of Year 7.

Once all cash receipts and expenditures are forecast, the rate of return on the net capital investment, or *IRR*, can be calculated. (This procedure is well-explained in *The Appraisal of Real Estate* and most basic financial analysis textbooks.) In the example presented in Table 5.3, the *IRR* equals 20%, which includes a component for profit.

The project *IRR* is compared to the benchmark return requirements of the market. If the expected *IRR* of the project is greater than the benchmark requirement, the project may be considered financially feasible; if the *IRR* falls below the benchmark, the project may be financially infeasible.

Special Considerations

Two special considerations pertaining to a financial feasibility study must be noted: incremental analysis and the treatment of membership fees.

Incremental Analysis

To analyze the financial feasibility of modifying an existing facility such as adding a clubhouse, or another 18 holes, an incremental analytical technique is used. In an incremental analysis, the existing facility is used as the base line and its net cash flows are forecast first without the proposed modification. Then the cash flows of the entire facility are again forecast, this time

TABLE 5.3 FEASIBILITY ANALYSIS FOR PROPOSED 18-HOLE GOLF COURSE
(All figures are in thousands)

Item	Year 1	Year 2	Year 3	Year 4	Year 5	Year 6	Year 7
Rounds times	0	0	25	42	45	50	50
average daily fee	—	—	×$15	×$25	×$30	×$35	×$37
Total golf revenue	$0	$0	$375	$1,050	$1,350	$1,750	$1,850
Car rental	$0	$0	$75	$126	$135	$150	$160
Driving range	0	0	10	17	20	24	26
Golf shop sales, net	0	0	65	109	117	130	130
Food & beverage sales, net	0	0	76	151	168	188	205
Total net revenue	$0	$0	$601	$1,453	$1,790	$2,242	$2,371
Expenses, inflated							
Golf course	0	$200	$405	$420	$445	$465	$480
Pro shop	0	0	20	55	58	61	64
Food & beverage personnel	0	0	65	125	140	150	165
General & administrative	0	0	190	200	210	220	230
Other	0	0	45	50	53	60	65
Total expenses	0	$200	$725	$850	$906	$956	$1,004
Net operating income	$0	($200)	($124)	$603	$884	$1,286	$1,367
Plus: reversion value							
Cap rate (12.0%)							
Stable value							$11,392
Less: sales expenses (5.0%)							(570)
Reversion value	—	—	—	—	—	10,822	
Net cash flow	0	($200)	($124)	$603	$884	$12,108	$___
Less: capital expenditures							
Land cost	($1,000)						
Improvements	($3,500)	($800)	—	—	—	($500)	
Total capital	($4,500)	($800)				($500)	
Net project cash flows	($4,500)	($1,000)	($124)	$603	$884	$11,608	
Internal rate of return	20.10%						

Note: The net operating income of Year 7 is capitalized at the end of Year 6 to determine the reversion value in accordance with accepted valuation methodology.

with the proposed modification. The existing facility's annual cash flows are then subtracted from the modified facility's cash flows and the difference represents the net incremental cash flows attributable to the proposed modification. The internal rate of return to these incremental cash flows is then determined to ascertain the project's feasibility.

In incremental analysis it is important that the forecast analyze the entire facility with and without the proposal, not just the incremental income and expense of the project, because the possible impact of the proposal on other project operations must be considered. Consider a project to develop a clubhouse with full food and beverage service on a facility that previously had only a snack bar. In addition to the cost to construct the clubhouse and the income it will generate, one must also consider the possible diminution of income to the snack bar and even the potential cost to remove it.

Table 5.4 illustrates an incremental analysis for a $525,000 expansion of a facility. The expansion will increase the project's annual net operating income by $75,000 per year beginning one year after construction begins. Based

TABLE 5.4 INCREMENTAL FEASIBILITY ANALYSIS

Existing Facility	Year 1	Year 2	Year 3 Stable	Year 4 Reversion
Net operating cash flow	$500,000	$525,000	$550,000	$580,000
Capital expenditures	0	0	0	0
Annual cash flows	$500,000	$525,000	$550,000	$580,000
Plus: reversion*	0	0	4,592,000	
Net cash flow (A)	$500,000	$525,000	$5,142,000	
Facility as Proposed				
Net operating cash flow	$500,000	$600,000	$626,000	$655,000
Capital expenditures†	(525,000)	0	0	0
Annual cash flows	($25,000)	$600,000	$625,000	
Plus: reversion	0	0	5,185,000	
Net cash flow (B)	($25,000)	$600,000	$5,810,000	
Incremental cash flow (B-A)	($525,000)	$75,000	$668,000	
IRR, proposed	20%			

*Reversion at Year 4 annual cash flow: reversion capitalization rate of 12.0% less 5% sales expense.
†Payment for the proposed expansion project is made at completion of construction, which is assumed to be at the end of Year 1.

on a 20% *IRR*, the expansion idea is a good one and a detailed proposal should be prepared.

Club Membership Fees

Club membership fees and any similar prepaid fees which entitle the payer to future benefits must be given special attention. Depending on the fee, the service offered, and the terms and conditions of the agreement, specific and unusual legal conditions and obligations may apply to the disposition of funds in a cash flow analysis. The opinion of legal counsel should be obtained. In some cases, these funds must be placed in an escrow or trust account until the benefits are received, and therefore may not be reflected in the cash flow analysis until that time.

MAXIMAL PRODUCTIVITY ANALYSIS (HIGHEST AND BEST USE)

The objective of a highest and best use study is to determine the property use, from among reasonably probable and legal alternative uses, that is physically possible, appropriately supported, financially feasible, and results in the highest present value (i.e., maximal productivity) of the property.[2] The following discussion addresses the maximal productivity aspect of a highest and best use study.

Productivity is typically measured by the internal rate of return to a project, especially for alternative proposed developments. This chapter has discussed how the *IRR* for a project is determined, beginning with site se-lection and project definition. To find the alternative use with the highest *IRR*, one merely redefines the site or project definition and repeats the pro-cess to estimate the resultant *IRR*. This iterative process is continued until the analyst is satisfied that the project configuration with the highest *IRR* has been defined.

The maximal productivity analysis is typically conducted for proposed projects to find the configuration or design that offers the greatest return to invested capital. Analyses are often conducted, for example, to determine

2. *The Appraisal of Real Estate*, 10th ed. (Chi-cago: Appraisal Insti-tute, 1992), 275.

whether or not to include a golf course in a residential development. The relative financial benefits of these alternatives are measured by estimating the *IRR* of the project both with and without a golf course.

This type of analysis is used by potential buyers of a golf course to determine which of several purchase opportunities offers the greatest financial reward. It is an essential part of any appraisal of a proposed or existing property for one must value a property at its highest and best use. For an existing golf course, other uses are often precluded by legal or physical constraints. The alternative uses typically considered involve alteration of the existing facility, which may include renovation, expansion, fee structure changes (e.g., from daily fee to private club), or a change of services (e.g., introducing swimming, tennis, lodging facilities). All alternatives are measured with a maximal productivity analysis.

Conclusion

Although the iterative process described may appear laborious, once a computer model is written for the first financial feasibility analysis, redefining the project and its model under different assumptions is relatively simple. The major components of this model are demand analysis, income projections, and cost estimates, which are required in most appraisal assignments anyway, so the construction of the model is relatively easy. Moreover, the number of alternatives can be reduced by drawing deductions from the factual data available—i.e., one would not consider building an expensive country club in a lower income area.

CHAPTER SIX

HIGHEST AND BEST USE ANALYSIS

 A golf facility must be valued at the most profitable, competitive use to which it may be put. Determination of this use constitutes highest and best use analysis. The highest and best use of a property is defined as:

> The reasonably probable and legal use of vacant land or an improved property, which is physically possible, appropriately supported, financially feasible, and that results in the highest value.[1]

A highest and best use analysis is conducted for the land as though vacant and the property as improved or, for a proposed project, the golf facility as proposed.

LAND AS THOUGH VACANT

The highest and best use of the land as though vacant assumes that the property is either vacant or can be made vacant by demolishing any improvements. The purpose of this analysis is twofold.

1. For vacant land, the analysis determines to what use the land should be put, that is, a golf course or another use. If a golf course is the highest and best use, the analysis will also specify the characteristics of the facility, including its size, quality, fee structure, and ancillary improvements.

2. For improved land, the analysis establishes the basis for land valuation in the cost approach and the estimation of depreciation. The study may indicate that the improvements contribute nothing to the land value and should be removed so the land can be put to better use.

In valuing the land for a use other than as a golf facility, the analyst must make sure that the impact of the subject site as a golf course is excluded from the value indications of comparable sales. For example, one may find that the value of the land as a golf course is $8,000 per acre while residential land in the neighborhood is valued at $25,000 per acre, and conclude that the highest and best use of the golf course as improved is for redevelopment as residential use. However, *without* the presence of the golf course the value of the subject site as residential land may decline to $15,000 per acre, and therefore change the previous conclusion.

PROPERTY AS IMPROVED

The highest and best use of the property as improved serves as the basis for all the approaches to value by identifying that use which will yield the highest value. For an existing facility, this analysis will determine if a greater value could be realized by changing the tangible or intangible characteristics

1. *The Appraisal of Real Estate*, 10th ed. (Chicago: Appraisal Institute, 1992), 275.

of the property, such as the size, condition or function of the improvements; the fee structure; or the services provided. For a proposed facility, the study will determine whether an alternative plan represents a superior use. If so, the property is appraised under these specifications. These specifications will also serve as the basis for identifying comparable properties to be used in the valuation process and for comparing their characteristics.

CRITERIA FOR ANALYSIS

Whether vacant or improved, the highest and best use of a property must meet four criteria. It must be that use that is: 1) physically possible, 2) legally permissible, 3) financially feasible, and 4) maximally productive.

Physically Possible

When analyzing the site as though vacant, the physical characteristics of the land are often a major determinant as to the uses to which it may be put. Often a golf facility can make use of a site's unique physical characteristics, which may limit other uses. For example, a site subject to occasional flooding, earthquake hazards, or a lack of access or exposure may have a lower value for residential or commercial uses, while these factors have little effect on a golf-related use. As discussed in Chapter 2, however, a golf course has specific physical requirements in regard to size, irrigation, soil quality, topography, climate, and other environmental aesthetics that must be met. The physical characteristics of a site affect the possibility of its use as a golf facility and must also be carefully considered in determining the type of facility to be developed.

The highest and best use as improved must also be a use that is physically possible. Any proposed changes to existing improvements must be capable of being accomplished. It is, however, usually the site as though vacant which ultimately restricts the physical possibility of a use because existing improvements can be demolished if they interfere with a considered use.

Legally Permissible

Any use considered for the property must be legally permissible. Private restrictions, zoning requirements, and environmental regulations must be identified because they can preclude many potential uses. Due to the size, high public visibility, and community impact of a golf facility, use decisions are often controversial and political. Increasingly, environmental concerns place restrictions on the use of land. Whenever a change in use is considered, the appraiser must investigate legal and political factors. Potential limitations on use are not usually clearly defined; substantial research may be required to determine the likelihood of gaining approval for a proposed use.

Financially Feasible

Financial feasibility relates the capital investment required to achieve a specified use and the income that will be realized from that use. Financial feasibility analysis was discussed in Chapter 5, which introduced the internal rate of return (*IRR*) as the measure of the relationship between investment and income. A proposed use is considered feasible if the *IRR* meets or exceeds the benchmark yield requirements of the market.

Maximally Productive

Several different uses may be feasible—i.e., produce an *IRR* equal to or greater than a typical investor's criteria—but the use that offers the highest *IRR* is maximally productive. If this use meets the other three criteria, it represents the property's highest and best use.

It is important to remember that the use with the highest *IRR* is the maximally productive use only if its level of uncertainty and risk is equivalent to that of the alternative uses considered. Uncertainty relates to the likelihood of an outcome, while risk relates to the level of loss or reward associated with an outcome.

Consider two alternative uses, each with an *IRR* of 15%. One investment has a 95% probability of meeting or exceeding this *IRR*, the other has an 85% probability. The first use, which has greater certainty, would most likely represent the highest and best use. If, however, the first project requires an investment of $15 million and the second requires only $5 million, the situation becomes more complicated. The uncertainty remains equivalent, but the risk is different, so the choice for highest and best use is less clear. Probabilistic forecasting and risk analysis, which addresses such a situation, is beyond the scope of most appraisal assignments and of this text. Uncertainty and risk are relevant to the appraisal process, however, so the appraiser should be familiar with the concepts.

At a minimum, when comparing alternative uses, the income and expenses of all alternatives must be forecast with the same level of certainty. If the most likely income level is projected for one alternative, while the income of another is projected conservatively, the basis for effective comparison is eroded.

HIGHEST AND BEST USE AND THE APPROACHES TO VALUE

The highest and best use determination serves as the bridge between factual data on the subject property and its environment and the valuation process. Based on the characteristics of the subject and its environment, one determines the highest and best use to which the subject may be put. The property is then valued at that use.

Chapters 7 through 9 address the three approaches used to estimate value: the cost, the income, and the sales comparison approaches. In the cost approach value is estimated by determining the cost to develop an equivalent facility, including land, and deducting the depreciation evident in the subject property. Because it is founded on the principle of substitution and replacement sites are usually impossible to procure, this approach has limited usefulness. The income approach assumes that value is based on the price the market would pay to receive the future income that the subject property will produce. In the sales comparison approach value is estimated by analyzing prices paid for similar, comparable properties.

Typically all three approaches are employed and each yields a value indication. These three value indications are then reconciled into a final opinion of value. The appropriateness and accuracy of each approach depends on the characteristics of the subject property, the purpose of the assignment, the quantity and quality of data available, and the valuation methodologies used by investors in the subject's market. Based on these criteria, the appraiser may conclude that one approach is less appropriate than the others, and exclude it from the analysis. More commonly, all three approaches are employed and when their value indications are analyzed, they are weighted based on the above criteria and reconciled into a final value estimate.

SPECIAL CONSIDERATIONS

Municipal Facilities

In valuing a municipal facility, one must consider its benefit to the public, which is often not reflected in its financial performance. The facility must be valued at its highest and best use, which may be a privately owned daily fee course rather than as a municipal facility. The difference between its value in use as a municipal course and its highest and best use value represents its public benefit value. The public body served by the project must determine if the benefits produced by the course are equal to the dollars invested. This concept is demonstrated in the following example, in which the sales comparison approach is used to value the facility using a greens fee multiplier as the unit of comparison.

TABLE 6.1 CALCULATION OF PUBLIC BENEFIT

	As Municipal Course	As Daily Fee Course
Annual rounds	70,000	50,000
Average greens fee per round	× $10	× $20
Annual greens fees	$700,000	$1,000,000
Greens fee multiplier	× 5.0	× 5.0
Value	$3,500,000	$5,000,000
Public benefit	$1,500,000	

Operated as a municipal course, the property has a value of $3.5 million based on its 70,000 annual rounds and $10 average fee. If it were operated for profit as a privately owned, daily fee facility, a $20 fee could be charged, which would reduce the rounds to 50,000, but increase the value to $5 million. Therefore, the fair market value of the course is $5 million, while its value as a municipal course is $3.5 million. The municipality has in essence underwritten the $1.5 million difference as a public benefit. This benefit is realized by those playing the additional 20,000 rounds which would otherwise be denied them, presumably because they could not pay a $20 fee.

The highest and best use of this facility may be deemed its present use as a municipal course if the public believes the recreational benefits it receives are worth $1.5 milion. If not, the course could be sold for $5 million, its market value.

Proprietary Nonprofit Facilities

The appraisal of a proprietary nonprofit facility involves considerations similar to those described above. Instead of a public benefit, a proprietary nonprofit course produces a membership benefit. Again, the facility is appraised at its highest and best use, which may be another use considering the criteria of maximum productivity.

In certain appraisal assignments, notably a study of value in use, a value other than that of highest and best use may be called for. In these cases the limited use being valued must be clearly specified.

CHAPTER SEVEN

COST APPROACH

 The cost approach is uniquely applicable to the appraisal of golf-related facilities. The approach estimates represent the cost to develop a property. When applied to a golf course, the cost approach includes a valuation of all of the elements of the enterprise, including, but not limited to,

- Land
- Improvements such as irrigation and drainage systems trees, greens, tees, fairways, service roads, golf car paths, bridges, and lakes
- Buildings such as clubhouse, maintenance buildings, and miscellaneous structures
- Personal property such as maintenance equipment, office equipment, clubhouse furniture, pro shop fixtures, and golf cars
- The liquor license
- Intangibles (also referred to as *business value*) attributed to the facility's reputation or name, in-place factors such as trained staff and management, a unique design, and the membership list.

APPLICABILITY OF COST APPROACH

Traditionally, the cost approach has been accorded unusual weight in the valuation of a golf course because golf courses are considered special-purpose properties that were not frequently exchanged in the market. Potential buyers, therefore, would focus on the cost of replacing the facility minus an allowance for recognized depreciation. As will be seen, the appraisal of a golf course is extremely complicated and frought with potential errors. An understanding of the entire process is needed to provide guidelines for analysts.

Many golf facilities, especially country clubs, are not profit-oriented ventures and, therefore, income capitalization techniques have limited applicability. (For a dicussion of the three approaches to value as they relate to nonprofit courses, see Chapter 10.) The lack of a profit motive and the scarcity of golf course transactions, which are needed in the sales comparison approach, suggests that the cost approach must be emphasized. This approach is especially important when the project is new and the market feasibility study supports the objectives of the investment. Investment objectives rather than economics or projected cash flows are considered because many golf courses are created to support investment objectives of a surrounding project and boost residential subdivision sales or resort revenues.

In valuing a resort-related course, the concept of use value may be applicable. *Use value* is defined as "the value a specific property has for a specific use."[1] A use value appraisal virtually always results in a conclusion of value greater than the perceived market value. The appraiser must be extremely careful in defining the scope and purpose of the assignment so as to not confuse use value with market value.

Golf facilities that are subject to the monetary controls and play restrictions set forth in a homeowner's association's covenants, conditions, and restrictions (CC&Rs) are limited-market properties. Use value or market value may be applicable to these valuations depending on the purpose of the appraisal. The cost approach is of particular importance in determining use value.

Specialized appraisals assignments often rely on the cost approach. A purchase price segregation and remaining life study performed for tax purposes is entirely based on depreciated cost estimates of the physical assets. (For a discussion of allowable lives, see Chapter 10.) Similarly, an appraisal for insurance purposes is derived from a separate valuation of the insurable components of a golf course.

Finally, a study of costs is essential to the determination of financial feasibility, in which the analyst estimates the *IRR* of a proposed golf course or an addition to an existing facility. Financial feasibility is indicated when a golf course's net present value exceeds its development costs, exclusive of any allowance for entrepreneurial profit.

The cost approach assumes that a project is complete, but the definition of *complete* is subject to misinterpretation. There is a difference between a physically complete project and a financially, operationally complete project. Failure to recognize this distinction can result in a market value estimate that does not include consideration of development cost factors such as fill-up or membership sales costs and fees, negative cash flows during the development and marketing phases, and the possibility of higher-than-normal interest rates or related holding costs until permanent financing is achieved.

SPECIAL SITUATIONS

Buyers of profit-oriented golf courses rarely use the cost approach to estimate an acquisition price. Sellers of these properties rarely apply the approach either, although some may. However, when a golf course is slated for redevelopment, the approach may be applicable because an accurate land appraisal based on various highest and best use scenarios is the primary valuation determinant. The appraiser performing such an assignment need not have golf course experience unless parts of the existing course—i.e., land or improvements or a combination of both—are to be retained and incorporated into an adaptive reuse plan. In the sale of a large and inefficiently designed golf property that is to be reconfigured and rerouted, for example, excess land may be developed or sold to capitalize on the golf course amenity.

Transactions involving the sale of land approved or expected to be used only for a golf course are extremely rare. Such a situation involves a complicated adjustment process and a land value estimate derived by the cost approach would be quite difficult and somewhat speculative in nature. At best, only a highly experienced appraiser should undertake this challenge. More likely, the cost approach should be used in this situation only as a check on the other approaches. Cost and depreciation estimates for most physical assets should not present a problem, but compiling a complete,

1. *The Appraisal of Real Estate*, 10th ed. (Chicago: Appraisal Institute, 1992), 22.

valid estimate of the value of intangibles is a task that requires special training.

An appraiser should always recognize that a golf course is first and foremost a business enterprise operating in a real property environment. Many appraisers of golf facilities overlook the business enterprise component or confuse it with the value of the real estate, making the land residual to the value indicted by the economics of the project. It is essential that all the contributing elements of a golf course be properly identified, especially in an appraisal for mortgage lending and real property taxation purposes. In both of these cases the business enterprise element receives special treatment. The lender is primarily interested in the security provided by the physical assets; the local assessing body is prohibited from taxing the intangibles.

APPRAISING A GOLF COURSE SITE

When the continued operation of the golf course or country club is the highest and best use of the property, land value should be derived from sales of land that is specially approved or to be used only for golf course purposes. This is difficult to do because these transactions are scarce. In circumstances where undeveloped land zoned or planned for low-density residential or mixed residential use can also be considered for golf course use, it may be appropriate to use these types of transactions, with proper adjustments, to estimate land value. When a golf course is slated for redevelopment to alternative land uses, the assignment is not golf-related and the comparables should be derived from other sources.

In ad valorem appraisal assignments involving nonprofit clubs, statutes may dictate that certain types of land sales be used. For most appraisals the problem is finding an adequate number of applicable transactions. The problem is compounded by the fact that many golf course land transactions involve a combination of proposed land uses, so the analyst must separate each component through an allocation process which may involve a complete appraisal of the comparable. This option should be avoided at all costs except when there are no sales or ground leases of golf course land to capitalize.

The first step in the land appraisal is understanding and categorizing the site characteristics. Critical factors include surrounding land uses; topography; the availability of utilities, especially water; access and location; and site shape. Less important are easements, zoning (if golf is an allowed use), views, and vegetation. It is recommended that an adjustment grid be used for comparison.

Land prices are usually expressed on a per-acre basis, but they may also be compared on the basis of a site value or price. A number of estimates should be made, if possible, to arrive at a land value conclusion. Rules of thumb or tests should also be utilized. One rule of thumb is use of a greens fee multiplier whereby the golf course land is valued by multiplying the typical or average greens fee by a factor derived from an analysis of golf land transactions in which greens fees are known. This calculation is illustrated as follows:

Proposed greens fee for subject	$5.00
Factor derived from golf course sales in region	×100,000
	$500,000

In this example the factor of 100,000 was derived by analyzing three sales of golf course sites. The average price of these sites was $808,000 and the average greens fee was $8.00 at the time of sale ($808,000/$8.00 = 101,000, or 100,000). Because the subject course has an average greens fee of $5.00 on the date of the appraisal, the land is less valuable than the comparable sites. Sole reliance on this technique is inadvisable; other adjustments should always be considered. A detailed analysis of comparable land sales is recommended (see Figure 7.1).

FIGURE 7.1 SUMMARY OF GOLF COURSE LAND SALES AND COMPARATIVE ADJUSTMENTS

Comp. No.	Location	Date	Acres	Holes	Price per Acre	Adjusted for: Time*	Topo†	Location‡	Other§	Total Adjust- ment	Ad. Price/ Acre
Subject	Semi-private course at outskirts of town	4/91	139	18	—	—	—	—	—	—	$3,600
1	Newly completed course in adjacent community	2/89	126	18	$5,200	$5,920	-0-	-35%	-0-	0.65	$3,848
2	Nearby course on crowded site	3/86	91	18	$2,500	$3,389	-0-	-0-	+5%	1.05	$3,558
3	Par-3 course in developed area	7/89	27	9	$4,900	$5,441	+5%	-20%	-0-	0.85	$4,625
4	Land that is part of mixed-use project	2/90	380	27	$2,950	$3,163	-0-	+5%	+20%	1.25	$3,954
5	Major course in same community	6/82	160	18	$1,300	$2,206	-0-	-0-	+60%	1.60	$3,530
6	Raw land at rural fringe	12/90	275	18	$1,790	$1,835	+10%	+20%	+60%	1.90	$3,486

Property Characteristics
Subject. Developing area; completed in 1988.
Sale 1. Superior demographics; sold with all approvals.
Sale 2. Same influences as subject; sold with entitlements, but without final approval.
Sale 3. Small course near apartment projects; had other potential land uses.
Sale 4. Slightly less desirable location; buyers thought golf land as valuable as land for other uses.
Sale 5. Good comparable, but old transaction; sold without any entitlements.
Sale 6. Inferior location; excess land to be sold for subdivision; no entitlements.

Value Conclusion
Sale 3 was disregarded due to its small size and differences in the financial aspects of the operation. The other sales range in value from $3,486 to $3,954 per acre. The best comparable is Sale 2. The value conclusion is $3,600 per acre, or $500,000.

Adjustment Notes
*Time adjustment is 6% per year or 0.5% per month, compounded.
†No adjustment for level or rolling land; varied adjustments for steeper topography or elongated shape.
‡Location or market adjustments reflect qualitative difference in sites as reflected by demographics and fee structure.
§Other adjustments reflect stage of entitlements at date of sale. Transactions with positive adjustments lacked various approvals at time of sale.

In analyzing sales of land that eventually evolved into golf course or country club projects, it is extremely important to determine the state of project approvals at the time of purchase. In many jurisdictions the approval process can take years and involve enormous legal and consultant fees, holding costs, management time, and overhead expenses. Purchases of unapproved raw land (i.e., sites without proper zoning or entitlements) can be misleading and must be properly adjusted. The entire spectrum of costs that separate raw land prices from approved project prices can be quantified on an itemized basis, but the total cost still may not represent the difference in value between a parcel of land without entitlements and one with a site or building permit. Acreage that has all the necessary approvals often increases in unit value by hundreds of percentage points, especially in communities where there is a scarcity of developable land or where growth restraints are common. The adjustment grids prepared by appraisers must account for the significant differences in stages of development or approvals that separate raw land comparables and a golf course site. Rules of thumb or land adjustment factors (e.g., approvals increase raw land acreage by a factor of 1.6) derived from an analysis of actual developments may be applicable if supporting transactions are available.

In some jurisdictions golf course land prices may be expressed on the basis of price or value per hole. This system is appropriate when land sales derived from 9-hole, 18-hole, 27-hole, or larger projects are analyzed. Comparisons of per-acre prices for smaller and larger projects may be unreliable because prices are apt to vary based on size factors alone. Other factors that can significantly affect land prices are open-space dedications, land use restrictions, utility easements or lines, and mineral rights. A comparison grid for analyzing golf course acreage transactions is shown in Figure 7.1.

Restrictive land use designations, covenants, or deed restrictions may be significant to the appraisal if market participants are considering possible alternative uses for a golf course in the future. Such a situation might arise in relation to an urban course surrounded by extremely high-priced residential and commercial land uses. However, for a golf course with no likely alternative use potential, comparison with golf course land transactions subject to restrictive planning or other zoning overlays may be entirely proper.

Utility easements for underground cables or overhead lines may be a significant problem for residential or commercial projects, but appear to pose no problem for golf courses. The routing of fairways and the placement of tees and greens can be adjusted to accommodate these undesirable, but necessary, features of our environment; indeed, surface uses, landscaping, paths, and other site improvements are typically allowed within utility rights of way. A talented architect can conceal or work around these features so they do not detract from the course design or appearance or represent an undue hazard. Similarly, mineral rights can produce royalty income without interfering with the golf course activities; such rights would be a special addition to the land value.

Golf course land value may also be estimated by capitalizing projected land rental income. Discounting is applicable if the income stream is irregular and especially if the project is in a growth stage. Capitalization of land rental income is especially applicable in valuing public or municipal courses because the analyst can examine the leases of operators who have developed golf projects on publicly owned sites. Land rents are typically based on a percentage of the gross incomes generated by the course's revenue-producing departments. The net present value of the annual estimated land rental income can be used as evidence of a golf course's site or acreage value in the appraisal process. This type of analysis is shown in Figure 7.2.

Due to the difficulty of estimating the land value component of a golf course, the appraiser should consider a variety of techniques when comparable sales are unavailable. Land sales for golf course developments in far-removed locations may be properly considered if the market dynamics are similar and they can be adjusted without applying unreasonable assumptions. It may also be proper to consider older sales in locations that are closer to the subject course.

FIGURE 7.2 LAND VALUE ESTIMATE BY CAPITALIZED INCOME FROM GROUND LEASE (18-HOLE PUBLIC COURSE)

Revenue Estimates at Stabilized Play

Category	
Green fees	
Weekdays	$420,000
Weekends & holidays	340,000
Discount play	110,000
Subtotal	$870,000
Other fees	
Golf car rental	$192,500
Driving range	22,500
Subtotal	$215,000
Total golf income	$1,085,000
Departmental income	
Food sales	$115,000
Beverage sales	70,000
Shop sales	130,000
Total departmental income	$315,000
Gross income	$1,400,000
Estimated Land Rents	
Golf related revenues @ 20% of $1,085,000	$217,000
Departmental revenues @ 4% of $315,000	12,600
Total annual land rent	$229,600
Valuation of Golf Course Site	
$229,600 capitalized @ 10% =	$2,296,000

Note: For a 160-acre site, this value equals $14,350 per acre; all property expenses are the responsibility of the lessee.

COST ESTIMATES: SOURCES AND TECHNIQUES

The difficulty encountered in applying the cost approach to unique properties typically lies in the estimate of replacement cost. The problem is magnified by the technical nature of golf course improvements. Most appraisers are unfamiliar with golf terminology and data sources. The glossary and bibliography provided at the end of this book will provide readers with additional information.

Sources of golf course replacement cost estimates include published construction cost manuals, computer cost services, course builders and architects, and trade publications. Cost manuals with special sections on golf courses include *The Boeckh Building Valuation Manual*, published by American Appraisal Company, and *Marshall Valuation Service*, published by Marshall and Swift. Appraisers may also have access to special valuation monographs prepared by state agencies for use by assessors and boards of equalization.

Unit Costs

Most replacement cost figures are reported in typical ranges for various quality classifications. For example, *Marshall Valuation Service* lists unadjusted costs in four quality classifications for regulation courses (see Figure 7.3).

The cost manual warns users that individual course costs can vary sub-

FIGURE 7.3 COST RANGE PER HOLE

Regulation Courses

Class I. Minimal quality, simply developed budget course on open natural or flat terrain, few bunkers, small tees and greens ..... $35,000 − $46,000

Class II. Simply designed course on relatively flat terrain, natural rough, few bunkers, small built-up tees and greens, some small trees .... $47,000 − $63,000

Class III. Typical private club on undulating terrain, bunkers at most greens, average elevated tees and greens, some large trees moved in or clearing of some wooded areas, driving range .. $64,000 − $86,000

Class IV. Championship course on good undulating terrain, fairway and greens bunkered and contoured, large tees and greens, large trees transplanted, driving range, name architect .... $88,000 − $120,000

Short Courses

Pitch and putt course. 9 holes on 10 to 15 acres, 1,000 yards long, including irrigation, excluding structures and lighting .... $17,000 − $23,500

Par-3 course. 9 holes on 15 to 20 acres, 1,400 yards long, including irrigation, excluding structures and lighting .... $22,000 − $30,000

Executive course. 18 holes on 50 to 60 acres, 4,800 yards long, rated par 60, including irrigation, excluding structures and lighting .... $30,000 − $39,000

Source: *Marshall Valuation Service* (Los Angeles: Marshall and Swift, 1991).

stantially from the stated ranges and that it may be appropriate to adjust items included in the cost-per-hole pricing by analyzing individual unit costs. It states that "Primary variables in golf course costs are type of terrain, size and layout, amount and quality of irrigation systems and overall quality. Excluded from these ranges are extensive grading, such as required for canyon and hillside courses, special drainage problems, all structures including bridges, and lakes. Included in the cost per hole are normal clearing of land including incidental grading, complete irrigation and drainage systems, planting of trees in open land, greens, tees, fairways, service roads and cart paths, financing during construction, and architect's fees."[2]

Readers of this book are advised not to apply any of the foregoing base prices or price ranges to a golf course valuation assignment; further adjustments are necessary for time and location. For example, using the cost manual, a project in Evanston, Illinois, would require upward adjustments of .05 (time) and 1.15 (locale) to be applicable to an assignment during the spring of 1991. An appraiser should obtain a copy of the appropriate cost manual and be familiar with all required assumptions and adjustments before arriving at any conclusion regarding replacement cost.

More accurate golf course cost estimates can be derived by applying unit or segregated costs rather than cost-per-hole figures.

Detailed Cost Estimates

In all valuation assignments, except those in which preliminary recommendations are made, it is wise to use itemized unit costs or contractor's estimates. Unit costs may be difficult to obtain, however, because sources of published data on golf course reproduction and replacement costs are limited. Appraisers should consult golf course maintenance superintendents, golf course architects, and contractors who specialize in the development

2. *Marshall Valuation Service* (Los Angeles: Marshall and Swift, 1991), section 67, page 1, May 1989.

of golf courses to obtain actual cost data and specifications for improvements such as irrigation lines that are underground and cannot be measured. An example of a typical cost estimate used by a developer is shown in Figure 7.4. Such a cost estimate shows direct costs only.

Indirect Costs. The direct costs of a project can be obtained from golf course contractors or subcontractors. Indirect costs are general to the project and do not fall into any category of direct costs. Such costs include financing costs, fees, or points; interim interest; utility costs; and special community fees for utility connections, traffic improvements, and schools. Building permit fees are generally included in direct costs.

Developer's Overhead and Profit

In the cost approach an allocation must be made for entrepreneurial effort and economic motivation. Depending on the type of operation, developer's overhead and profit may be as important in a golf course valuation as it is in appraisals of commercial property. Its applicability is doubtful in the development of nonprofit courses in which a suitable allowance may be made for management expense in the development process if this function is not performed by a committee.

A theoretical discussion of development and appraisal is beyond the scope of this text. Nevertheless, appraisers should attempt to quantify an appropriate charge for developer's overhead and profit by investigating the practices of golf course development organizations.

ESTIMATING DEPRECIATION

To derive a market value estimate using the cost approach, depreciation is deducted from the replacement or reproduction cost of the improvements. The depreciation attributable to a golf course may be physical, functional, or external in nature.

Depreciation factors unique to golf courses include constant exposure to the elements, application of chemicals (e.g., pesticides, fertilizers), and extensive physical contact (e.g., golf cars on fairways, clubs bashing tees and fairways, players trampling on vegetation). Many components of a golf course have much shorter useful lives than components of commercial property. Land improvements generally depreciate at more than twice the rate of building improvements.

Methods

Formulas can be used to calculate total golf course depreciation, but techniques such as the economic age-life method are rarely appropriate and their results should be considered speculative. A sales comparison analysis should be conducted if suitable golf course sales transactions are available, which is unlikely. Income capitalization techniques may be applicable, but are sometimes oversimplified. However, they may provide guidance as to the amount of investment required to maximize the financial potential of a course.

Because the physical components and useful lives of golf courses can vary widely, the breakdown method of estimating accrued depreciation is recommended. To apply this method the appraiser must measure each cause of depreciation separately. This analysis is useful to both the preparer and the user of an appraisal because it provides a detailed study of the condition of all physical elements of the facility. The process may be conducted using a checklist of common defects (see Figure 7.5) and should result in distinct

FIGURE 7.4 COST ESTIMATE FOR PROPOSED 18-HOLE PROJECT

Code	Description/Unit Costs	Total Cost	
10	Engineering and surveying	$20,000	
	Design fee—golf course architect	175,000	
	Architect's expenses	15,000	
	Irrigation design fee	26,000	
	Construction management	60,000	
	General and administrative	20,000	
	Subtotal for consultants		$316,000
20	Utilities (electrical power installation to operate wells, pump station, and office)	$50,000	
	Utility installation (to pumphouse and maintenance facility)	20,000	
	Water source (fee for water rights)	25,000	
	Pump station	100,000	
	Intake and enclosure (intake valve and pipe: $10,000; pump station enclosure: $35,000)	45,000	
	Irrigation system (100 acres with 3 parallel lines, sprinkler head, outlets, connections, etc.)	960,000	
	Irrigation repairs (repairs and parts for irrigation system following installation)	10,000	
	Subtotal utilities and irrigation		$1,210,000
	Finish grading (final grading; greens, tees and bunker construction)	$500,000	
	Cleaning/trash removal	10,000	
	Lake construction		
	Stage 1	$72,000	
	Stage 2	60,000	
	Stage 3	101,000	
	Stage 4	43,000	
	Subtotal major site work		$786,000
30	Lake transfer lines (10" pipe, fittings, valves and installation)	25,000	
	Car paths (4' wide; 11/2" asphalt over gravel base)	84,000	
	Sand bunkers	40,000	
	Parking lot	42,500	
	Drainage	150,000	
	Subtotal for course and land improvements		$341,500
40	Seed (cost of fairway seed @ $18,000 and costs of greens seed @ $2,000)	20,000	
	Fertilizer/chemicals	94,000	
	Stolons (estimated for 50 acres of fairways and 3.5 acres of tees; stolons plus hydromulch)	117,500	
	Trees	200,000	
	Plants	40,000	
	Fumigation (dependent on greens design; use methyl bromide)	20,500	
	Greens material (estimated @ 9,100 tons of sand and 2,570 tons of gravel)	127,000	
	Subtotal for ground cover/landscaping		$619,000
50	Labor/wages (18 months of development)		
	Laborers	596,000	
	Mechanics	35,000	
	Irrigators	53,000	
	Foremen	75,000	
	Leadmen	34,000	
	Subtotal for labor and wages		$793,000
60	Equipment rental	30,000	
	Equipment repair	25,000	
	Small tools and supplies	20,000	
	Fuel	15,000	
	Golf course accessories (e.g., flags, poles, cups, trash cans, ball washers, benches, tee markers, trap rakes, etc.)	25,000	
	Subtotal for equipment, etc.		$115,000
	Total golf course costs		$4,180,500

FIGURE 7.5 VALUE-DECREASING DEFECTS

Tees

- Area is too small.
- Surface is uneven or poorly sloped.
- Sides are so steep that hand maintenance is required.
- Soil is too heavy, making compaction a major problem.
- Vegetation and trees provide too much shade and restrict air movement.
- Poor access for golfers creates adverse traffic patterns and paths or worn turf.
- Location of tees is hazardous; golfers risk being hit by errant golf shots.
- Poor drainage impedes play and causes compaction.

Roughs

- Pasture-like surface may be bumpy and full of holes and weeds.
- An abundance of trees, brush, or rocks complicates maintenance.
- Undrained wet areas cause play and maintenance problems.
- Clumpy and thin turf results from an unsuitable seed mix.

Hazards

- Positioning requires a long "carry" over the water or short lay-up shots.
- Weeds and algae create eyesores.
- Bunkers are too tall, too steep, and weed-infested, making them hard to maintain.
- Traps are too flat and not visible.
- Poor drainage causes traps to hold water.
- Difficult shape impedes maintenance.
- Location is handicap for average golfer.
- Sand is hard-packed or contains stones.

Greens

- Greens not elevated for visibility; merely a closely mowed area.
- Slope is improper, either too steep or allowing pockets that trap water.
- Soil structure is incorrect. Too much clay causes compaction problems; too much sand causes leaching problems; rock in the subsoil interfere with cup placements; improper soil mix depth causes localized dry spots.
- Landscaping or trees block sunlight and hinder air movement.
- Steep side banks cause maintenance problems.
- Poor approaches create traffic wear.
- Putting area is too large or too small.

Fairways

- Improper drainage hinders playability.
- Lack of width makes play overly difficult.
- Excessive roughness causes difficult lies, bumps, or unpredictable bounces of the ball.
- Soil is too hard, so a divot cannot be taken.
- Boundaries are poorly defined, confusing the golfer about direction of play.
- Poor bridges or steep hills make movement difficult or hazardous.
- Outcroppings of rocks damage clubs and mowing equipment.
- Poor turf increases maintenance requirements and impedes play.

Source: *Golf Courses: A Guide to Analysis and Valuation* (Chicago: American Insitute of Real Estate Appraisers, 1980), 41, 44–47.

estimates for curable and incurable physical deterioration and curable functional obsolescence. Incurable functional obsolescence is rarely found and usually considered a minor item. External obsolescence is usually attributable to locational problems.

Curable Physical Deterioration

Items of deferred maintenance can be identified through consultation with the golf course superintendent. This type of depreciation would be measured as the cost of replacing items such as worn out and leaking irrigation lines or the cost of reseeding fairways. For buildings it could be measured as the cost of roof repairs and a paint job. These and other observed conditions are considered curable if the cost of correcting the problem would be offset by an equal or greater increase in value. Minor items of physical deterioration do not always require individual treatment and may be provided for in a lump-sum deduction.

Incurable Physical Deterioration

As a general rule, all physical defects in golf course improvements can be corrected. Thus, depreciation due to incurable physical deterioration should typically be applied only to the structural elements of the clubhouse and related buildings after the cost to cure deferred maintenance items has been deducted. A detailed explanation of the treatment of long-lived and short-lived building components is beyond the scope of this text. Incurable physical deterioration is calculated with the physical age-life method by applying the ratio of effective age to estimated total physical life separately to the reproduction or replacement cost of each short-lived and long-lived building component affected.[3]

Curable Functional Obsolescence

Obsolete golf course design results in loss of value. Problems in routing, hole lengths, inappropriate or misplaced hazards, and the placement of the tee or hole can damage the status of a facility and have a negative effect on its potential revenue. Courses can be redesigned to eliminate undesirable features or to attract a different type of player. Many older courses have been altered a number of times to increase their competitiveness and renew their image. The principles governing curable functional obsolescence also apply to the clubhouse and other buildings.

Input from technical experts is needed to analyze and quantify golf course design deficiencies. Determining the economic benefits of correcting deficiencies is exceedingly difficult and involves projecting future revenues and operating expenses. For discussion and examples of curable functional obsolescence in buildings, readers should consult general valuation texts such as *The Appraisal of Real Estate*.

Many golf course appraisal assignments deal with the valuation of an existing golf course or country club after an expansion and modernization program has been completed. In these instances the size and design inadequacies of the property are being corrected and the added value of the investment is reflected in the appraisal of the completed facility. No estimate of functional depreciation is necessary unless other deficiencies remain.

If a course is being appraised "as is," an appropriate allowance for depreciation attributed to design problems must be made. "To be curable, the cost of replacing the outmoded or unacceptable aspect must be the same or less than the anticipated increase in value."[4] The two steps required in this depreciation estimate are 1) determination of feasibility and 2) estimation of the loss in value. Figure 7.6 illustrates the estimation of depreciation due to functional obsolescence.

In the example shown in Figure 7.6, the golf course is being penalized for more than the immediate cost of improving three holes because of the detrimental influence on total course income attributed to the undesirable

3. *The Appraisal of Real Estate*, 10th ed. (Chicago: Appraisal Institute, 1992), 348–352.
4. Ibid.

FIGURE 7.6 CALCULATING DEPRECIATION DUE TO FUNCTIONAL OBSOLESCENCE

1. Determination of Feasibility

Cost to eliminate undesirable features of three holes	$350,000
Salvage value of irrigation lines and attachments	−50,000
Net cost	$300,000
Potential increase in annual rounds: 3,500	
Potential gain in annual revenue (3,500 rounds × $20/round)	$70,000
Less increase in maintenance costs and taxes	−$15,000
Gain in net operating income	$55,000
Increase in course value ($55,000 capitalized @ 12%)	$458,333

2. Estimation of Depreciation

Total replacement cost of golf course improvements	
($185,000/hole x 3 holes)	$555,000
Less physical deterioration already deducted	−375,000
Subtotal	$180,000
Plus net cost to improve	$300,000
Loss in value	$480,000

features that currently exist. This oversimplified analysis is presented for illustrative purposes only. In the real world improvements for most of the golf course and some of the buildings are generally scheduled when a major renovation program is undertaken.

External Obsolescence

Off-site influences that can reduce the value of a golf course in the current market are limited in nature, number, and quantitative effect because there is a strong demand for golf. The strong, unsatisfied demand for golf can also overcome and diminish other forms of golf course depreciation.

When external obsolescence does exist, it may be identified with the underperformance of a golf course in comparison with more successful facilities in the market area. External factors that can detract from a golf course's income-producing potential generally relate to locational factors such as poor demographics or an inadequate number of golfers within the appropriate income categories. In a few instances, notably in some Sunbelt communities, there is excess competition.

Although external obsolescence attributable to market dynamics is incurable on the part of the owner or operator, it may diminish over time as the target population grows or as positive changes occur in golf participation and frequency of play.

External obsolescence is often identified in courses built in newly developed subdivisions or residential communities where the population levels necessary to produce revenues in excess of operating costs and debt service will not be reached for many years.

External obsolescence attributed to existing neighborhood conditions is rarely found outside of declining communities. Except in an undeveloped market that is in a growth stage, the depreciation attributed to outside forces is reflected largely in the land value estimate. When a golf course is badly located relative to potential and existing golfers, a full cost approach analysis should probably not be undertaken.

A deduction for external obsolescence due to market absorption is calculated in Table 7.1.

TABLE 7.1 CALCULATING DEPRECIATION DUE TO LOSS IN INCOME DURING ABSORPTION PERIOD

Year	Desired Rounds	Projected Rounds	Difference	Average Greens Fees	Lost Income	Discounted at 15%
1	30,000	25,000	5,000	$20	$100,000	$86,957
2	45,000	37,000	8,000	$22	$176,000	$133,081
3	50,000	48,000	2,000	$24	$48,000	$31,561
Total						$251,599
					Rounded	$250,000

FURNITURE, FIXTURES, AND EQUIPMENT

A detailed cost approach analysis could theoretically call for a depreciated replacement cost analysis of each item of furniture, fixtures, and equipment (FF&E). Such a detailed analysis may be excessive because of the time required to prepare an inventory, inspect each item, contact suppliers for cost information, and determine an appropriate deduction for all forms of depreciation. Since FF&E generally accounts for 3% to 9% of total golf course property and FF&E analysis is essential only in the cost approach, it is recommended that the appraiser apply one of the procedures described below to arrive at a reasonably accurate estimate of value for the entire category of personal property.

Book Value Method

The value imputed to FF&E can be taken from the golf course's balance sheet. This method is quick and easy, but produces doubtful results when the FF&E is older. It is most applicable when the items are new because the prices paid for the FF&E are current.

Modified Book Value Method

The first step in this method is to analyze the average age of the FF&E. Then the original cost of the entire group of assets is adjusted upward to a level that approximates the current replacement cost. Finally an average rate of depreciation is applied to the entire category of FF&E to arrive at an estimate of current market value.

Comparable Course Method

Cost information from newly developed courses with similar characteristics is anlyzed to provide an overall estimate of replacement cost for the course being appraised. An overall depreciation estimate is then applied to this total cost figure to indicate the current value of all items of FF&E. The overall depreciation percentage applied is a function of the average life expectancy and condition of the personal property and its effective age, which is determined by studying asset acquisition dates and maintenance records.

Asset Grouping Method

An average cost of replacement figure is derived for each revenue or expense department through consultation with department managers and the head accountant. These department costs are then individually depreciated using the same consultative process used to compile an accurate estimate of depreciated market value.

Of the four techniques just described, the asset grouping method is most accurate, followed by the comparable course method, the modified book value method, and the book value method. The method applied depends on the purpose of the appraisal assignment and the requirements of the client. Most appraisals can be completed in a satisfactory manner using one or more of these four techniques if the required cost data are adequately supported and the depreciation study is based on sound reasoning.

A detailed, item-by-item replacement cost and depreciation estimate for FF&E is beyond the scope of most golf course appraisals unless the client requires the information for asset management or tax purposes. (See Chapter 10 for information on valuation for price segregation.) If a detailed estimate is required, the real estate appraiser may find it necessary to consult a golf course equipment specialist.

Several principles must be considered in appraising FF&E. First, choose a method appropriate to the degree of accuracy required for the assignment at hand. Second, recognize that an overhead or installation cost factor should be added to most items to account for assembly. Third, provide a separate estimate of external obsolescence to be applied to the entire depreciated replacement cost figure if external obsolescence affects the value of the golf course as a going concern. Fourth, recognize the need for outside assistance from suppliers or other specialists when the available data are inadequate.

(A sample inventory of FF&E, by department, with estimated acquisition costs is included at the end of this text.)

APPRAISING THE BUSINESS COMPONENT

The intangible value of a real estate development that is operated as a business is, at times, ignored by real estate appraisers. Where intangible value exists and can be independently quantified, real estate appraisers often combine this element of value with the real property or tangible assets of the project and include it as part of the income approach. When comparable sales that include an intangible component are used for comparison, the business value of each sale price is often not segregated or separately identified, but is included as part of the value of the physical assets. These practices are unacceptable and in violation of accepted standards.

In applying the cost approach to a golf course facility, the appraiser must investigate and identify economic activities that create intangible value in addition to real and personal property values. It is not sufficient to conclude that the difference between the values estimated in the cost approach and the income approach can be attributed to business value or goodwill. As part of a golf course valuation and analysis, the appraiser should provide a separate estimate of the value of intangible factors so that the cost approach conclusion can be independently compared to the income approach conclusion and the business value component can be isolated in the comparable sales analysis.

The value of intangible assets is separately quantified and segregated for a variety of reasons, especially to establish a basis for mortgage loan security, depreciation schedules for income taxes, and ad valorem taxation. The appraisal assignment may be limited to preparing a purchase price segregation to be used by the owner's accountants in preparing state and federal tax returns. (A sample price segregation study and depreciation estimate for tax purposes is included in Chapter 10.) When a separate valuation of intangible assets is required, the expertise of a fully qualified golf course and country club analyst is needed.

Obviously a recreational facility that captures its operating revenues from golfers is a business activity operating within a real estate environment. A golf course's business value can include a variety of intangible assets and, if possible, these assets should *not* be aggregated into a single unit referred to as *goodwill*. Intangible assets can include permits and licenses, name or reputation, customer lists, management systems, management contracts and covenants not to compete, staff in place, supplier relationships, golf professional agreements, and tournament contracts.

Analyzing and individually valuing a complicated group of individual, intangible assets may be beyond the scope of most assignments. Nevertheless, an accurate technique must be available to the valuation practitioner. Intangible assets can be valued with the excess profits technique, analysis of sales of golf course business opportunities, the residual/segregated value technique, or the management fee technique.

Excess Profits Technique

The excess profits technique is a modified income capitalization process in which a stabilized net income figure is allocated between the real, personal, and intangible assets. The stabilized net income excludes annual cost factors not related to operations such as depreciation, amortization, and interest expense, but includes an appropriate annual allowance for *all* management functions, including that of the owner. The necessary and proper returns on all assets and the recapture of depreciating assets on an annualized basis are then deducted from the stabilized net income to yield the excess income attributed to the business. The calculations are shown in Tables 7.2 and 7.3.

TABLE 7.2 CALCULATION OF STABILIZED NET INCOME

Income Adjustments			Summary of Asset Value	
Taxable income		$222,500	Land	$500,000
Plus:			Golf course	$1,725,000
Depreciation	$167,500		Buildings	$1,200,000
Interest	$300,000		Equipment	$350,000
Inventory adjustment	$22,000		Inventory	$80,000
Minus:			Operating capital	$120,000
Owner's salary	$72,000		Liquor license	$30,000
Retirement plan	21,000			
Car expense	6,000			
Other personal	3,000			
Total adjustments		$387,500		
Stabilized net income		$610,000		

TABLE 7.3 DETERMINATION OF ASSET RETURNS AND RECAPTURE REQUIREMENTS

Asset Values	Return	Recapture	Portion of Net Income
Land: $500,000	10%		$50,000
Golf course: $1,725,000	10%	4%	241,500
Buildings: $1,200,000	10%	2.5%	150,000
Equipment: $350,000	12%	10%	77,000
Inventory: $80,000	14%		11,200
Operating capital and liquor license: $150,000	8%		12,000
Total required net income			$541,700
Stabilized net income			$610,000
Difference—net income attributed to business			$68,300

The final step in this analysis is to capitalize the excess profit of $68,300 into a value conclusion. The capitalization rate applied to an intangible factor is typically higher than the percentage returns on tangible assets. Assuming that a rate of 20% is indicated, the appraised value of the business component of the project would be $341, 500 ($68,300 ÷ 0.20). The full value of the golf course entity is summarized in Table 7.4.

TABLE 7.4 VALUE CONCLUSION

Asset	Value
Land	$500,000
Golf course	1,725,000
Buildings	1,200,000
Equipment	350,000
Inventory	80,000
Liquor license	30,000
Business enterprise	341,500
Total value	$4,226,500

Sales of Golf Course Business Opportunities

When golf course operations can be leased (e.g., from a local municipality), sales of the leasehold interest can be used to determine the business value of another golf course by developing multipliers such as those applied to sales or net income.

Following the previous example, assume that the rental expense for the real property asset on an annual basis is 25% of gross annual revenues, which total $1,600,000. Assume also that studies of other golf course leasehold transactions indicate that buyers are acquiring golf course business opportunities for 50% of their annual gross revenues, or four times their adjusted net incomes. Multipliers such as these should always be derived from actual sales transactions. Using the same asset values used in the previous example, except for the business component, a valuation range of $340,000 to $350,000 is indicated for the intangible assets. The calculations are shown in Table 7.5.

TABLE 7.5 VALUATION OF INTANGIBLES

Using annual income multiplier:	
0.5 × $1,600,000	$800,000
Less value of equipment, inventory & license	460,000
Net value of intangibles	$340,000
Using net income multiplier:	
Net income	$610,000
Less rent of 25% × $1,600,000	400,000
Net to leasehold operator	$210,000
Net income multiplier	×4
Total business value	$810,000
Less value of equipment, inventory & license	460,000
Net value of intangibles	$350,000

Residual/Segregated Value Technique

Assume that an appraiser has an assignment to appraise a golf course that has been recently acquired and the valuation analyses for the whole property support the indicated price. In this case it is acceptable to value the components of the property by the cost approach and assume that any residual amount is attributed to intangible factors or the business enterprise.

Management Fee Technique

A simplified technique that is sometimes appropriate involves capitalization of all or part of a management fee. Obviously, a basic or minimum management charge is necessary regardless of the profitability of a golf facility. In some circumstances, however, a particular management organization may produce operating returns that result in excess profits. The incentive fees paid to management for extraordinary performance are, in essence, a return on certain intangible services such as organization of personnel, management systems, public relations, and promotion. In other words, the payment of a management fee can result in a higher level of performance than is found at golf courses of a similar character. The problem with calculating intangible value with this methodology is the ill-defined relationship between the amount of the management fee and the extent of intangible asset values.

In some valuation assignments it is not necessary to isolate or to analyze and quantify separately the business component of a golf course or country club. The total value of the facility as a going concern is usually sought in circumstances involving transfer of ownership, gift or inheritance tax matters, and investment counseling and decision making. In other assignments (e.g., for mortgage financing) it is necessary to identify and appraise each of the individual assets of a golf course or country club.

CHAPTER EIGHT

INCOME APPROACH

 The income approach to value is based on the economic principle that the value of an income-producing property is the present worth of anticipated future benefits. The annual cash flow or net income projection is converted into a present value indication using discounting or capitalization. Methods of capitalization are based on inherent assumptions concerning the quality, durability, and pattern of the income stream.

Direct capitalization is performed by applying an overall capitalization rate to a single year's net operating income. This technique is appropriate for valuing an existing property when its current income equals or approximates the stabilized income level at fair market rates.

Sometimes the pattern of projected income is irregular as it is during the absorption period of a new or modified facility. An existing facility that has not reached stabilization or has become unstabilized due to internal or external causes may also have an irregular income pattern. In these cases a discounted cash flow (DCF) analysis, or yield capitalization, is most appropriate. When this method is applied, the present worth of future cash flow expectations is calculated by individually discounting each anticipated, periodic future cash receipt at an appropriate discount rate. The market value derived is the accumulation of the present worth of each year's projected net income plus the present worth of the reversion, or terminal value. The estimated reversion value, which is the forecasted property value at the end of the projected holding period, is based on direct capitalization of the projected net income in the reversion year.

Golf course income and expense categories should not be estimated based on industry averages, but on data from a variety of sources, especially comparable golf courses. Average performance data are presented in this chapter for the purposes of illustration.

APPLICATION TO GOLF FACILITIES

The theory, general practices, and methodology of the income approach can be applied to most property types, including golf facilities. The techniques are well documented in valuation literature and should be understood by any appraiser or consultant undertaking a golf course appraisal assignment.

The challenge to the appraiser lies in applying income approach principles to this unique property type. The most difficult task typically is acquiring the data required to make sound income and expense projections and determine appropriate discount and capitalization rates. To obtain current, specific information that corresponds to the unique characteristics of the subject facility, the appraiser must carefully select and verify primary data. Fortunately these data are generally available to appraisers who have developed successful interview techniques. Facility managers, for both private and publicly owned courses, are generally willing to share their data. Although gathering primary data may seem difficult at first, with experience an appraiser can develop contacts, a deep database, and the interview skills needed to yield excellent results.

There are several excellent sources for secondary data, including the National Golf Foundation (NGF) and the Professional Golfers' Association (PGA). At least one accounting firm publishes operating statistics for country clubs. Unfortunately, no one publication or source provides sufficiently comprehensive data to meet all the requirements of the income approach. Appraisers must consult several sources to accumulate data. The data available may be general in nature, lack timeliness, and be unsuitable as the sole basis for valuation, but they can be valuable in specific instances and as general indicators.

NGF and PGA regularly conduct national surveys of the income and expense experience of golf facilities. Detailed data on each of the income and expense categories discussed below are available from these sources. Because this information is regularly updated and voluminous, it is not stated here. Some of these data will, however, be used for specific examples and discussion purposes. A summary of revenues and operating expenses on a percentage distribution basis taken from a recent PGA survey is included in the appendix at the end of this text.

Validity

The income approach is the most commonly used, and typically the most accurate, measure of value for golf facilities. It reduces the differences between courses to the least common denominator, net income, which is quantified in the market and converted into value through the application of a market-derived capitalization rate. A golf facility is typically acquired for its income-producing capacity, and the income approach directly measures this important attribute.

Some appraisers maintain that the income approach is not appropriate for facilities that are not profit- or income-oriented. Such facilities include proprietary private clubs that provide golf as an amenity to the surrounding real estate development and publicly owned facilities. The nonprofit orientation of a golf course is, however, only the structure elected by the current owner. The facility's future income potential can still be measured with a profit-oriented analysis to produce an accurate and appropriate value indication. (A full discussion of this topic is presented in Chapter 10.)

STRUCTURE OF THE APPROACH

The income approach consists of five basic steps:

1. Select an appropriate projection period.
2. Forecast gross revenues.
3. Forecast annual operating expenses.
4. Select appropriate discount and capitalization rates.
5. Apply proper discounting and capitalization procedures.

Projection Period

Projection periods generally range from one to 10 years. The period should extend until the property's net income stream is expected to stabilize, which occurs when demand, or rounds played, prices, and expenses become relatively constant. In projecting future revenues and expenses, past results should be carefully considered; negotiations with potential purchasers typically focus on the seller's last operating statement.

One-year projection periods are appropriate for existing facilities which have achieved stabilized income. Direct capitalization is applied to the stabilized net income to arrive at an estimate of value.

Projection periods for proposed facilities (and existing facilities with unstable income patterns) typically range from three to 10 years from the completion of construction. This period may reflect the typical absorption period for golf facilities or a client's requirements. A project with an absorption period of more than five to seven years is frequently infeasible unless it represents a phased development, in which a longer absorption and projection period is warranted. The projection period should extend one year beyond stabilization.

If, for example, a project has a four-year absorption period after construction is completed and stabilization is expected in Year 5, Year 6 will also be projected. The premise is that Year 6 will serve as the basis for determining the reversion value of the facility in the direct capitalization of its income. The reversion value is presumed to be realized in Year 5 as proceeds of a hypothetical sale of the facility. The value of the project at completion of construction is, therefore, the present value of the cash flow benefits (and deficits) realized over the four-year absorption period plus the fifth year's stabilized operating cash flows plus the proceeds of reversion.

Projection periods of more than 10 years are rarely used in the valuation of golf facilities. However, they may be necessary if a facility is subject to a ground lease that is due to expire or influenced by other factors that will change the expected income within the foreseeable future. The ultimate use of the appraisal, particularly when the payment of debt service is critical, may make it necessary to employ a longer projection period.

Projecting absorption periods for golf facilities is a difficult and imprecise process. Although the absorption period extends until stabilized income is achieved, this point in time almost always coincides with stabilized demand. Thus demand analysis, which was discussed in Chapter 5, forms the principal basis for determining the absorption and projection period. (When the time of stabilization is affected by factors other than demand, such as changes in price or operating expenses, the duration and effect of these factors are usually well known.) In estimating the absorption period for a facility, the appraiser should consider:

- The absorption periods of comparable projects
- The results of the demand analysis
- The subject's competitive position
- Specific primary data on absorption such as focus group studies or market surveys
- Extent of the marketing campaign
- The golf-related experience of the developer and facility management

Market experience shows that absorption is not constant. Demand increases fastest in the project's early years and tapers off as the facility nears stabilization.

Table 8.3 on page 95 shows a discounted cash flow analysis for a proposed 18-hole, daily fee facility. Although this analysis would be modified to reflect the idiosyncrasies of the course being appraised, its basic structure is applicable to any golf course.

GROSS REVENUE

Gross revenue may be derived from a number of sources depending on the products and services offered by the specific facility. These sources are grouped into two general categories for discussion purposes: course utilization income and ancillary income.

Course Utilization Revenue

Course utilization income represents revenues received from the use of the golf course itself. This income may be generated through daily fees or course memberships. These two fee structures may operate separately or simultaneously.

The term *daily fee* typically refers to the payment of a prescribed fee for use of the course a single time. Within this general structure there are usually several fee categories, which may include general use, weekend and weekday play, twilight hours play, seniors, juniors, shoulder seasons, local residents, or others. These fees may be set at differing rates and are commonly called *greens fees*.

A course membership purchased by a golfer entitles the member to certain use privileges of the golf course. These privileges typically include unlimited use with no greens fee or a reduced greens fee for all rounds played over a prescribed time period. This time period varies and may cover a year, a summer, the member's lifetime, the period of residence in the neighborhood or at the on-site hotel, or until the grantor of the membership (the course owner) sells the course.

In exchange for membership, the member will typically pay both a fee and dues. The membership fee is a one-time entry charge; member dues are periodic payments, usually monthly or quarterly. Occasionally other payments are required. One common type of fee is a minimum periodic food and beverage charge. If the member spends less than a set amount on food and beverages at the facility during a prescribed period, he or she is billed for the difference.

There are typically two types of memberships: proprietary and nonproprietary. A proprietary membership grants the member a partial ownership interest in the facility. Although this is usually permanent, it may be some other interest such as a lifetime estate. A proprietary membership may be revocable. With rare exceptions, the membership fee generated through the sale of proprietary memberships cannot be considered a source of revenue in the income approach to value because it does not constitute income to the owner, but rather a sale of a portion of the ownership interest in the property. Note, however, that in the determination of highest and best use, the analyst may find that maximum productivity would be realized by selling subdivided interests in the facility under a proprietary membership structure. This determination is made primarily through a special and cautious application of the income approach.

A nonproprietary membership grants the member certain use privileges of the facility, but no ownership interest.

Treatment of Course Utilization Income

The gross income forecast typically begins with a forecast of course utilization revenue. First the income structure to be used by the course must be determined. This determination is typically based on the highest and best use and represents the structure that demonstrates maximum productivity. For example, the highest and best use of an existing facility operated on a daily fee basis may be conversion to a nonproprietary private club. In this case, the course utilization income structure analyzed must be that of the subject as a private club.

Alternatively, to apply the income approach to a proprietary facility that does not have a profit objective, one must first assume that the proprietary members sell the facility. Then highest and best use analysis is performed to determine the course utilization income structure which yields maximum productivity, and the facility is valued under that structure to find the income it will generate for a buyer.

Utilization income from all sources must be recognized. Frequently various utilization income categories must be considered. For example, a private club may generate utilization income not only from membership fees and dues, but also from guests or reciprocal privileges which generate daily greens fees.

To demonstrate the preparation of a gross income forecast a simple daily fee course utilization structure will be assumed in the following discussion. If, however, a membership structure is indicated, three special factors should be considered.

1. *Nonrecurring income.* Do not capitalize nonrecurring income unless the membership is nonproprietary. Specifically, initiation fees are a one-time revenue item which must be excluded from direct capitalization. (For exceptions, see *turnover fees* below.)

2. *Turnover fees.* Turnover initiation fees are generated when memberships are resold. They are commonly recurring and may be capitalized. A membership club usually sets a limit on the number of memberships it will sell. Once this capacity is reached, no new membership sales will occur. However, when an existing membership is discontinued, it may be resold. This may or may not generate revenue to the facility. If the membership is fully transferable with no transfer fee, the member may sell the membership personally and retain the proceeds. However, if the membership is nontransferable, or if there is a transfer fee, revenue will be realized by the facility upon transfer. There is usually some turnover of memberships, and this generates recurring annual revenues which must be included in the projection. Often a regular turnover rate of a certain percentage of the membership base may be determined based on the subject's history, the experience of comparable facilities, and demographic and market trends.

3. *Services included.* The services included in a membership must be considered. For example, members may be entitled to free lockers and discounts on car rental, while daily fee players pay full price. This must be factored into ancillary income projections.

Course Utilization Revenue Projection

The course utilization revenue projection is the product of the forecast demand times the price. The methodology for determining demand and price was presented in Chapter 5. Briefly stated, one sets a price (project description), measures demand at this price (demand analysis), and determines the

IRR (feasibility analysis). Then a new price is assumed and the process is repeated iteratively until the *IRR* is maximized (highest and best use).

To demonstrate the projection of course utilization revenue and expenses in the income approach, a hypothetical, typical course called City Links is presented as an example. A complete income approach analysis of this course is summarized in Table 8.3 on page 95. The City Links Golf Course is a proposed 18-hole, daily fee facility offering full services. The value to be determined is the value at completion of construction, assumed to be current at the date of the appraisal report.

A utilization revenue forecast for City Links is presented in Table 8.1. This forecast is based on a demand analysis which projects that stable operations will be achieved in Year 4; Year 5 is projected to serve as the basis for the reversion value. Demand is measured in annual rounds played and greens fees, as well as all subsequent dollar forecasts, are expressed as actual, inflated dollars.

TABLE 8.1 CITY LINKS GOLF COURSE: GREENS FEES INCOME FORECAST

Year	Annual Rounds	Greens Fee	Annual Revenue
1	20,000	$20	$400,000
2	35,000	$24	$840,000
3	38,000	$26	$988,000
4	40,000	$28	$1,120,000
5	40,000	$30	$1,200,000

Ancillary Revenue

The second major category of revenues is ancillary revenue, which include all revenues from sources other than course utilization. Ancillary revenues, which are derived from a number of sources, may exceed course utilization revenues. Ancillary revenues may come from all or some of the following sources: golf car rental, driving range, food and beverage sales, pro shop, and other sources—e.g., tournament fees, instruction, locker and equipment rental, miscellaneous. These categories represent common sources of ancillary revenue, and each is addressed below.

Increasingly, golf facilities include complementary revenue centers such as lodging accommodations, conference and meeting facilities, and facilities for tennis, swimming, or horseback riding. These revenue sources and their valuation are beyond the scope of this text. However, if they constitute an integral part of the golf facility analyzed, they can significantly affect demand, course fees, and the scope of services projected.

Golf Car Rental

Golf cars are rented by the seat (i.e., one or two riders to a car) or by the car. The appraiser must be aware of the rental basis when surveying comparables and forecasting revenues. The simplest and frequently most appropriate unit of measure and comparison is to express car rental revenue as a function of rounds played. To calculate revenue per round, total car rental revenue is divided by the total number of rounds played. This is an appropriate measure when car revenue is directly related to rounds played, which is usually the case. The forecast figure is then simply the car revenue per round rate times the annual forecast of rounds played. It is sometimes more appropriate to estimate the actual percentage or number of rounds to be played with a rental car and multiply that estimate by the rental price.

Golf car utilization can vary substantially. Less than 20% of golfers may use cars on short, inexpensive courses in moderate climates, but more than 75% may use them on long, expensive courses in hot climates. A large and growing number of facilities require cars.

In our City Links example, rental revenue will be forecast at $4.00 per round, increasing 5% per year for inflation. This rate was determined using the demand analysis for this service.

Driving Range Revenue

Driving range revenues are affected not only by the number of rounds played on a course, but also by factors such as range quality (e.g., mat or grass surface, level or sloped range), price, and proximity to population centers. Therefore, gross revenues are typically estimated in terms of the total revenue per range.

In this example, assume that demand analysis demonstrated stabilized revenues of $25,000 per year in current dollars for the driving range, increasing at an inflationary rate of 5% per year. Assume also that absorption would be 75% stabilized in Year 1, 90% in Year 2, and 100% in Year 3, outpacing the absorption of the golf course due to a greater level of unmet demand.

Food and Beverage Revenue

Virtually all golf courses offer some food and beverage service, ranging from vending machines or a snack bar to top-quality restaurants, cocktail lounges, and catering service. Food and beverage sales may constitute a major portion of total revenues, more than 50% in some cases. The unit of comparison for daily fee facilities is usually dollars per round, while for private country clubs it is usually dollars per member. According to the national data available, food and beverage revenue averages $2 to $3 per round for daily fee courses and many times higher for private facilities. This revenue source usually varies directly with the number of rounds played on a daily fee course and with the total membership of a private facility.

For the City Links golf course, food and beverage revenue is forecast at $2.00 per round, increasing 5% per year for inflation.

Merchandise Sales

Merchandise sales are generated through the sale of goods such as golf clubs, balls, and accessories. With rare exceptions, merchandise customers have come to play a round of golf and the purchase of merchandise is incidental to this purpose. Therefore, revenue in this category is usually directly related to the number of rounds played and is projected based on merchandise sales dollars per round. This unit of measure is used for comparison with other facilities.

As a retail business, sales per round is influenced by factors such as the disposable income of the patrons, competition, management skill, and the character of the golf facility. Although the national mean is $2.50 to $3.50 per round, this figure can be misleading due to the wide variance among facilities. Certain high-profile courses with strong name recognition can generate substantial revenue, sometimes more than $10.00 per round, through the sale of products carrying their name or logo.

Merchandise sales are forecast at $2.50 per round, increasing 5% per year for inflation.

Other Revenue

Other revenue is often generated through lessons, club rental and repair, pro shop services, tournament fees, and miscellaneous sources such as telephone and locker rentals. Although each of these categories is relatively minor, collectively they may be substantial. Each of these categories, with the exception of tournament fees, is closely related to the volume of play, and therefore revenues are projected per round. In the City Links example, other revenue is forecast at $1.50 per round, increasing 5% annually.

OPERATING EXPENSES

Most operating expenses are routine expenditures necessary to produce the facility's gross income. Operating expenses are estimated on a cash basis and do not include expenses unique to a particular type of management, debt service, depreciation, interest, or income taxes. When the direct capitalization technique is used, one-time expenditures and capital expenditures are excluded; these are reflected in the reserves for replacement account. When the discounted cash flow technique is used, capital and one-time expenditures are shown in the period in which they are to be incurred; no account is usually made for annual replacement reserves except in the reversion year.

Operating expenses have three components: fixed expenses, variable expenses, and reserves for replacements, including capital and one-time expenses. (See Table 8.2.)

TABLE 8.2 EXPENSE SUMMARY

	1989 National Average*
Fixed Expenses	
Maintenance	$499,000
Personnel	105,000
General and administrative	58,000
Golf cars	17,000
Driving range	5,000
Total fixed expense	$684,000
Variable Expenses	
Merchandise	74% of sales
Food & beverage (cost of goods & personnel)	96% of sales
Food, cost of goods	43% of sales
Beverages, cost of goods	27% of sales
Food & beverage, cost of goods	38% of sales

*These national averages were compiled from surveys and samplings conducted by the Professional Golfers' Association and Pannell Kerr Forster. Course-by-course variances from these figures and percentages can be significant. These averages are used for the purpose of illustration only. Valuation data should be based on the expense history of comparable facilities.

Fixed Expenses

Fixed expenses are those that vary little, if at all, with the volume of demand for, or use of, the income source they support. Major categories of fixed expenses include course maintenance, personnel, general and administrative, golf car, and driving range expenses.

Course Maintenance

Course maintenance costs are nearly always one of the largest expense categories of any golf facility. A 1989 national sampling of country clubs indicated an average cost of $499,000 to maintain an 18-hole facility. However, maintenance costs vary widely, so generalizations are unreliable. Maintenance costs depend on factors such as the course location, climate, length of season, intensity of play, type of facility, size, and indicated quality of maintenance. This last factor is especially significant because any amount of money can be spent to keep a course immaculately groomed and maintained. Skilled management must determine an apropriate level of maintenance—i.e., the level at which an additional dollar spent will not generate an equivalent return. An experienced appraiser with good judgment should be able to forecast a reasonable expenditure for course maintenance. The best source of information is the golf course superintendent.

Personnel

Personnel expense is usually the next largest fixed expense. This category typically includes the cost of all personnel required for facility operations except maintenance and food and beverage personnel costs which are shown in separate departmental accounts. The personnel account covers payroll, payroll taxes, and employee benefits.

Personnel costs are affected by factors such as local labor rates, level of service, facility size, length of season, and management skill. The average personnel expense in 1989 was approximately $105,000.

General and Administrative

This account includes administrative expenses for office operation, insurance, utilities (except course maintenance utilities such as irrigation), phone, postage, travel, accounting, legal consultation, dues, subscriptions, automobile use, and miscellaneous other costs. Personnel is excluded. This expense averaged $58,000 nationally in 1989.

Golf Car

Expenses related directly to golf car rental operations include energy, maintenance, and cleaning. These expenses vary somewhat with utilization, but experience demonstrates that variance is low due to routine maintenance requirements. This expense averaged $17,000 in 1989.

Driving Range

Driving range expenses are generally fixed. The most variable component of this expense is replacement of golf balls, which amounts to approximately 10% of the total expense. In 1989 the average national expense for a driving range was approximately $5,000.

Variable Expenses

Variable expenses are those that vary significantly with the volume of demand. There are two major categories for a typical facility: merchandise and food and beverage expenses.

Merchandise

Merchandise expense consists of the actual cost of the goods sold. This category usually excludes personnel who perform other services in addition to selling the merchandise. Although the average 1989 merchandise expense was 74% of sales, this percentage may vary widely, especially for high-profile courses that sell products with course identification or logos at a substantial profit.

Food and Beverage

Food and beverage expense may be divided into two components: the cost of goods (food consumed) and personnel. Combined, these components usually total 85% to 100% of sales or more. Although food and beverage profit margins are low, the service is usually necessary. Management may not be

skilled in this aspect of business and sales volume is low by restaurant standards, but prices cannot be set too high or they will create feelings of goug-
ing and ill will. In 1989 the average combined food and beverage expense
was 96%. Often, especially during the absorption period of a proposed facility, it may be necessary to forecast the cost of goods sold and personnel
expenses separately; a certain personnel level is required to provide the basic level of service desired, regardless of volume. This personnel expense is
often estimated based on the actual number of employees required for each
projection period and their wage rates. The cost of goods sold is directly
variable and can be forecast as a percent of sales. In 1989 food costs averaged 43% and beverages 27%; combined they amounted to 38% of sales.

Replacement Reserves and Capital Expenditures

In addition to normal operating expenses, a golf facility will sometimes incur
capital expenses and other one-time expenses. Capital expenses usually relate to the repair or replacement of capital improvements with economic
lives shorter than that of the facility. These include items such as irrigation
systems, golf cars, and the clubhouse carpet, paint, and roof. One-time expenses may be incurred for unusual legal fees or promotional programs. A
thorough discussion of how these expenses are treated in the income approach is contained in the Appraisal Institute's textbook *The Appraisal of
Real Estate*. The size of the account for replacement reserves and capital
expenditures depends on the size, quality, and condition of the facility. In a
discounted cash flow analysis, these expenses are itemized and projected
individually for each future period in which they will be incurred. In direct
capitalization (and sometimes in the reversion year of a DCF analysis), they
are amortized into equal annual "payments" as in a reserves account.

Expense Forecasting

Itemized expense forecasts should be prepared for each major category of
fixed and variable expenses. These expenses are then forecast to estimate
a reasonable level of expense necessary for the subject to operate at its
highest and best use under competent management. When the actual expense history of the subject is available, it usually serves as the basis of this
forecast. It is adjusted for indicated changes in management, highest and
best use, and economic and market conditions.

These adjustments will be based on data gathered from actual cost estimates for labor, materials, and outside services, the expenses incurred by
comparable facilities, the opinions of knowledgeable professionals such as
club management personnel or golf course consultants, and secondary survey data. These data will also serve as the basis for expense projections
when an expense history of the subject is unavailable, as in the case of a
proposed facility.

The appraiser must exercise care when comparing the subject's expenses to expense data from other sources to ensure that consistent accounting practices are followed. Accounting practices vary considerably. For
example, the food and beverage expense reported for one facility may include related personnel expense, while another facility may include this expense in the personnel expense for the total facility. The appraiser must
carefully analyze each item to prevent double counting or the omission of
any expense items.

An expense forecast for the hypothetical City Links course has been pre-

TABLE 8.3 CITY LINKS GOLF COURSE: DISCOUNTED CASH FLOW ANALYSIS

Item	Year 1	Year 2	Year 3	Year 4	Year 5
Gross revenue					
Greens fees					
Rounds	20,000	35,000	38,000	40,000	40,000
Fee/round	× $20	× $24	× $26	× $28	× $30
Total greens fee	$400,000	$840,000	$988,000	$1,120,000	$1,200,000
Golf car rental	80,000	147,000	167,580	185,220	194,481
Driving range	18,750	23,625	27,563	28,941	30,388
Food and beverage	40,000	73,500	83,790	92,610	97,241
Merchandise sales	50,000	91,875	104,738	115,763	121,551
Other revenue	30,000	55,125	62,842	69,457	72,930
Total gross revenue	$618,750	$1,231,125	$1,434,513	$1,611,991	$1,716,591
Expenses					
Fixed operating					
Maintenance	$390,000	$430,000	$490,000	$600,000	$640,000
Personnel	95,000	105,000	115,000	127,000	134,000
General & admin.	58,000	61,000	64,000	67,000	70,000
Golf car	14,000	16,000	18,000	20,000	20,000
Driving range	4,000	5,000	6,000	6,000	7,000
Total fixed	$561,000	$617,000	$693,000	$820,000	$871,000
Variable operating					
Merchandise	37,000	67,988	77,506	85,664	89,947
Food & beverage					
Cost of goods	15,200	27,930	31,840	35,192	36,952
F&B personnel	43,000	45,000	51,100	53,700	56,400
Total variable	$95,200	$140,918	$160,446	$174,556	$183,299
Total operating expense	$656,200	$757,918	$853,446	$994,556	$1,054,299
Net operating income	($37,450)	$473,208	$581,067	$617,435	$662,292
Capital exp. (reserves)	$0	$0	$25,000	$15,000	$35,000
Net operating cash flow	($37,450)	$473,208	$556,067	$602,435	$627,292
Plus: reversion value					
Reversion cap rate					12.00%
Stabilized value					$5,227,430
Less: sales costs (3%)					$156,823
Reversion value				$5,227,430	
Net cash flow	($37,450)	$473,208	$556,067	$5,829,865	
Discount rate 16.0%					
Discount factor	0.8621	0.7432	0.6407	0.5523	
Present value	($32,284)	$351,670	$356,249	$3,219,783	
Net present value	$3,895,417				

Note: *NPV* figures were calculated by computer using more precise discount factors than are shown here.

pared using the national averages and the procedures presented here. This forecast is summarized in Table 8.3.

Net Cash Flow

Net cash flow represents annual gross revenue minus all expenses and capital improvements (replacement reserves) and excluding debt service.

Discount and Capitalization Rates

Discount and capitalization rates are factors that reflect the relationship between annual cash flows and present value. Again, the reader is referred to *The Appraisal of Real Estate* for a thorough discussion of related concepts and procedures.

Capitalization Rate

A capitalization rate represents the relationship between one year's net income and the property's present value. The capitalization rate, expressed as a decimal factor, is divided into the net income and results in an estimate of value by direct income capitalization.

Market value = net operating income/capitalization rate

Capitalization rates can be derived from studying comparable sales, analyzing the nature of golf facilities in relation to other property types, or using a band-of-investment technique. They can also be obtained through investment surveys and interviews with principals, developers, brokers, and lenders familiar with golf facilities.

Ideally, the capitalization rate used in the appraisal of a golf facility is derived from sales of comparable projects. Although capitalization rates generally range from 10% to 15%, rates are substantially affected by time, location, and the type and condition of the facility. For example, rates for trophy courses in parts of California were driven below 5% during 1988 and 1989, but these rates rose again in 1990 and 1991. The appraiser must be certain that the capitalization rate reflects, or is properly adjusted to reflect, stable income. (Many of the apparently low capitalization rates cited from golf course sales relate to properties where the market perceived income was not yet stable, and substantial future increases in income could be expected.)

The band-of-investment technique is based on the assumption that most properties are purchased with debt and equity capital and that each investment position requires a market-determined return on its investment. This return includes a competitive interest rate for the debt holder or lender and a competitive equity yield for the equity investor or developer. Band-of-investment calculations are illustrated below:

Component	Ratio	Rate	Rate Component
Mortgage	Loan-to-value ratio	× Mortgage constant	= Weighted average of debt
Equity	Equity-to-value ratio	× Equity dividend rate	= Weighted average of equity
			Overall capitalization rate

Typically, high loan-to-value ratios of 65% to 80% make capitalization rates very sensitive to mortgage conditions. When the mortgage market is active and information is available, the difficulty is in estimating an equity dividend rate that reflects the risks and intensive management associated with golf investments. Again, this information ideally should come from comparable sales or the individuals cited above as sources of capitalization rates. Therefore, the process is usually better accomplished by analyzing comparable sales, although the band-of-investment technique can serve as a useful check on the reasonableness of the rate chosen.

Finally, the appraiser must assess the advantages and disadvantages of the subject property and the duration and risks of its income stream relative to market-indicated rates to determine the appropriate capitalization rate for the subject property.

Discount Rate

A discount rate is a rate of return on capital used to convert future payments or receipts into present value. It should be market driven, i.e., derived from sales of comparable facilities. Another method of derivation is to add the inflation rate or annual compounded growth rate to the capitalization rate. This technique assumes that cash flow and the reversionary value will increase at the projected inflation rate.

It is not appropriate to estimate a discount rate until all inflationary assumptions have been determined and the cash flow model has been completed. If no adjustments for inflation are included in the projection, then the discount rate is the same as the capitalization rate. In a typical DCF analysis in today's market, discount rates will range from 14% to 18%. Because of their greater risk, proposed facilities typically have higher discount rates than existing courses. Investor surveys of yield rates are available to appraisers, but this information is frequently outdated. The best data are derived from the analysis of recent golf course transactions.

SAMPLE APPLICATIONS

Table 8.3 on page 95 shows a discounted cash flow analysis of City Links, the hypothetical, proposed, 18-hole daily fee facility that has been described and discussed in this chapter. Table 8.4 illustrates the direct capitalization approach, using the same facility but assuming it is currently operating at a stabilized level.

TABLE 8.4 CITY LINKS GOLF COURSE: DIRECT CAPITALIZATION APPROACH

Item	Year 1
Gross revenue	
Greens fee rounds	40,000
Fee/round	×$25
Total greens fee	$1,000,000
Golf car rental	160,000
Driving range	25,000
Food and beverage	80,000
Merchandise sales	100,000
Other revenue	60,000
Total gross revenue	$1,425,000
Expenses	
Fixed operating	
Maintenance	$499,000
Personnel	105,000
General & administrative	58,000
Golf car	17,000
Driving range	5,000
Total fixed	$684,000
Variable operating	
Merchandise	74,000
Food & beverage—cost of goods	30,400
F&B personnel	46,400
Total variable	$150,800
Total operating expenses	
Capital expenses (reserves)	$25,000
Total expenses	$809,800
Net operating cash flow	$615,200
Capitalization rate	12.00%
Value indication	$5,126,667

Business Value Component

The income approach as applied to the operations of a golf facility includes an allowance for the contribution of the business value component, if any.

In applying the income capitalization process, the appraiser should consider the unique risk, liquidity, and yield requirements for the intangibles that comprise the entire entity. In Chapter 7 the methodology for deriving the business value of a golf course was presented. The income approach can be used to appraise the assets of the entire facility as well as individual components such as intangibles.

CHAPTER NINE

SALES COMPARISON APPROACH

 A golf course, like a resort or hotel, is a unique grouping of facilities, amenities, and revenue-producing departments. No two courses are alike in terms of their physical characteristics, playability, reputation, social atmosphere, and other subjective criteria. Because of these differences, estimating the value of a course by comparing the prices paid for other properties is extremely difficult. Furthermore, unlike the other two valuation approaches, the sales comparison approach cannot be applied if no sales of golf courses are available to the appraiser. Data can be obtained through research, however, and many insights and secondary benefits can be gained from comparable sales investigations.

Except in unusual or required circumstances, the results of sales comparison analysis of a golf course should be expressed as a likely value range, not a single value estimate. This is accepted methodology in the appraisal of special property types and a realistic course of action considering the number of variables for which price adjustments may be required.[1]

The process of refining data and adjusting for differences between golf courses that have been sold and the property being appraised may be thought of as a continuum. As Figure 9.1 illustrates, the accuracy of the value estimate increases with the availability of data and the sophistication of analysis applied.

FIGURE 9.1 ACCURACY OF VALUE ESTIMATE

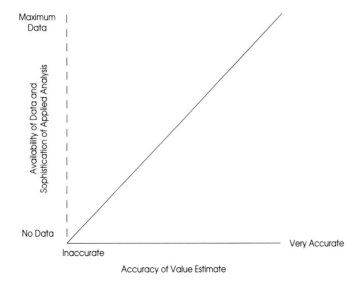

1. A list of approximately 50 items which could be considered in analyzing golf course sales comparables is provided in Chapter 10 in the discussion of non-profit golf clubs. In preparing a comparative analysis, the appraiser should consider all relevant factors that are significant to buyers and sellers. Adjustments should be limited to major categories of items.

Creativity in the analysis of golf course sales transactions should be encouraged, but the appraiser should remember to think about pricing and value in the same way that buyers, sellers, and brokers do.

The rules of thumb applied by knowledgeable market participants and more precise units of comparison used by appraisers are both derived from experience and investigation.

UNITS OF COMPARISON AND ANALYSIS

Most golf courses have 18 holes, so it would appear that the most common unit of comparison is price per course. However, in appraising short courses and facilities with 27 holes or more, it is common to convert sale prices into a price-per-hole figure. Thus, a 9-hole facility that was sold for $1,500,000 would have a price per hole of $166,667, and an 18-hole course that was sold for $3,800,000 would have a price per hole of $211,111. This information can provide a starting point for the analysis.

Golf courses with the same number of holes may have very different land areas due to a number of factors such as unusable topography, the configuration of fairways, the amount of natural vegetation, and natural waterways. These variables may not affect revenue, but they could have a negative influence on maintenance expenses if the course needs excessive watering or mowing. Thus, a value comparison based on price per acre is not recommended when appraising a golf course, whether it is existing or proposed.

Obviously, if the assignment is really an appraisal of a parcel of land that is improved with a golf facility but has another highest and best use, then the size of the land parcel is immensely important. In this case price per developable unit or price per square foot derived from appropriate comparable sales would be a proper unit of comparison. These units could also be applied to the excess land of a golf course that can be separately developed.

In most cases, however, units of comparison that relate to the financial aspects of a golf course transaction are preferred. When a substantial amount of data on recent golf course sales is available, the following indicators should be considered:

- Total revenue multiplier
- Golf revenue multiplier
- Price per round
- Price per membership
- Greens fee and rounds multiplier

The derivation, application, and validity of these factors should be understood because they can produce widely varying results. The calculation of these valuation indicators is illustrated in Figure 9.2.

Total Revenue Multiplier (*TRM*)

2. Gross income multipliers are used to compare the income-producing characteristics of comparable properties with those of the subject. Although the conversion of income into a value estimate is a capitalization process, multipliers are commonly applied in the sales comparison approach.

Most people in the real estate business recognize a gross income multiplier (*GIM*).[2] The multiplier is typically derived by dividing the sale price of a property by the total income produced by the facility during the most recent 12-month operating period. It is important to know whether the multiplier is derived from the 12-month period before or after the date of sale so that the multiplier can be applied consistently to the total income of the subject property.

A total revenue multiplier (*TRM*) can be applied to a golf facility. The

FIGURE 9.2 DERIVING UNITS OF COMPARISON FROM A GOLF COURSE SALE

Available Data
  Type: 18-hole, semi-private, regulation course
  Price: $4,226,500
  Rounds: 42,000
  Average greens fee: $18
  No. of members: 550
  Income (last fiscal year):

Greens fees	$756,000
Car fees	338,000
Driving range	47,000
Food & beverage sales	384,000
Pro shop sales	75,000
Total gross income	$1,600,000

Units of Comparison
1. Total revenue multiplier: $4,226,500 ÷ $1,600,000 = 2.64
2. Golf revenue multiplier:
         $4,226,500 ÷ ($756,000 + $338,000 + $47,000) = 3.70
3. Price per round: $4,226,500 ÷ 42,000 = $100.63
4. Price per membership: $4,226,500 ÷ 550 = $7,685
5. Greens fee and rounds multiplier:
         $4,226,500 ÷ 42,000 = $100.63 ÷ $18 = 5.59

advantage of the total or gross revenue multiplier is that it directly relates income production to sale price. The multipliers vary from property to property depending on the mix of departmental revenues and the relative profitability of each source of income. Where there is a large food and beverage operation, the multiplier will tend to be lower because the net income from these activities is usually only marginal. If the food and beverage operation of the facility is leased to a third party, the income component for this department declines greatly and, if all other revenue sources are the same, the multiplier will be substantially higher. If, in the example shown in Figure 9.2, the food and beverage operation were leased for 6.5% of the sales, the income to the total property would then be $1,241,000 ($1,600,000 − $384,000 + .065 × $384,000) and the total revenue multiplier would jump from 2.64 to 3.44.

Careful application of a total revenue multiplier can be very useful in valuation analysis. The problem with this technique is obtaining accurate revenue or income data. Moreover, if information about profitability is lacking or uneven, the interpretation of the value indication becomes unrealiable.

Golf Revenue Multiplier (*GRM*)

The amount of nongolf revenue generated by individual golf courses varies greatly and nongolf operations (e.g., food, beverage, pro shop, concessions sales) generally contribute relatively little to a facility's bottom line. Therefore, an appropriate multiplier should be derived only from direct golf activities such as greens fees, membership dues, car rental fees, and driving range fees.

Golf revenue multipliers (*GRMs*) should exclude initiation fees if they vary greatly from year to year. If they are a predictable source of annual revenue, they should be included. Food and beverage sales should always be excluded; pro shop sales may be included if the subject property has a significant pro shop operation. The advantages and disadvantages of using a golf revenue multiplier are the same as those associated with the total revenue multiplier.

Price Per Round (*PPR*)

It is often difficult to obtain financial statements for golf courses that have been sold. However, other statistics may be readily available from data-gathering organizations or obtained through investigation and interviews with knowledgeable parties such as club managers and golf pros. It is imperative that the annual number of rounds for a golf course be known to analyze a sale of the property.

The applicability of the *PPR* valuation indicator depends on other factors involved in the operation of a golf course, which must be analyzed and adjusted. Obviously, if a golf course is not realizing its maximum rounds potential because of poor management and marketing policies, the value estimate will be understated. Similarly, if greens fees at the comparable courses are very different from fees at the subject property, a problem will arise in the interpretation of the data. A refinement that adjusts for differences in greens fees and annual rounds played is described later.

Sometimes a price per round can be estimated for a group of golf course transactions involving similar properties with slightly different greens fees, but very different restaurant and shop facilities. Normally, if data are available to compute gross revenue multipliers, a reasonably accurate value range may be found. However, if financial data are not available, then some type of extra adjustment must be made to the valuation indicator. Valid adjustments for differences in building square footage can be made and their use is acceptable in contemporary appraisal practice.

The advantage of using a *PPR* estimate is that it can be derived from data that are readily available to experienced golf course analysts. The weakness of this indicator is that it does not provide for differences in the nongolf components of a course or the size and quality of amenities. It is most reliable when the comparables are very similar to the subject property in terms of fees and property characteristics.

Price Per Membership (*PPM*)

This valuation indicator is only applicable when the subject property is a private golf or country club and the comparables are also private or semi-private clubs. Price per membership is commonly used in the appraisal of racquet sports and health and fitness facilities because in these properties there is a direct relationship between the number of members, gross revenues, and net profit.

On the whole, private golf and country clubs are large, complicated investments and maintenance costs for the facilities are extremely high. They have varied classes of membership, which make comparisons difficult, and their marginal profitability diminishes the applicability of revenue multipliers.

The price per membership indicator can be used to explain the extremely high prices paid by Japanese investors for trophy golf courses. These buyers reportedly intend to recapture part of their acquisition costs by selling new memberships in the exclusive golf clubs to Japanese investors at inordinately high fees. As an example, the buyer of a new course in California plans to sell up to 1,000 new memberships to his fellow countrymen who will pay up to $50,000 for each membership—considered cheap by Tokyo standards. These sales should more than cover the $18,200,000 purchase price. Only time will tell whether this strategy is successful.

Greens Fee Multiplier (*GFM*)

A refinement to the price per round unit of comparison is the greens fee (and rounds) multiplier.[3] A variation of this methodology was described in Chapter 7 as a technique for valuing raw land. For a profit-oriented golf course, the greens fee multiplier can be a highly effective valuation tool. It provides a common denominator in the comparison of golf facility sales. Furthermore, it may be derived without access to financial statements.

The *GFM* is calculated by dividing the price per round, or *PPR*, by the average greens fee. This factor can be extremely important because it automatically accounts for variations in annual rounds attributed to different pricing policies among courses that appear to be comparable. For example, consider two courses in a common market area that vary in the number of annual rounds played by 30%. Sale 1 had 41,000 rounds with an average greens fee of $14 and Sale 2 had 28,700 rounds at an average greens fee of $20. Their *PPR*s would vary by 30%, but their *GFM*s would be identical because both courses had total revenues from greens fees of $574,000.

The problem in estimating a *GFM* is obtaining accurate data on average greens fees. Obviously, the most accurate figures come from financial statements, which may be difficult to obtain. However, careful questioning of club personnel and study of the various rates charged for weekdays, weekends, seniors, and juniors can help an appraiser derive a reasonably accurate figure.

It is recommended that this multiplier be used in all appraisals of profit-motivated golf course operations. The *GFM* accounts for pricing or qualitative differences between properties and is based on data that can be obtained by an accomplished analyst.

ADJUSTING GOLF COURSE SALES

When sufficient units of comparison are available from a golf course database, the appraiser should be able to derive an accurate value range. Up to five, separate valuation calculations can be made under ideal circumstances.

In a typical situation, an appraiser may find evidence of only a few recent, arms-length transactions involving golf courses over a large region; good, reliable data about sales are difficult to obtain. Quite possibly, detailed information may be available on only one or two transactions involving courses that are reasonably similar to the subject property.

When sales are scarce, the appraiser must conduct in-depth analyses of the few, good sales available to construct a convincing argument and account for all significant differences between the comparable sales and the subject property. The major physical differences between golf courses of a similar type can be identified using the golf course rating data described in Chapter 2.

A thoughtful study of a comparative golf course may reveal positive and negative cost factors that will account for property differences. For example, an estimate of the cost to improve fairways and greens, reconfigure the sprinkler system, or renovate the clubhouse of a comparable property could account for part of the variance in value or price between this course and the subject. Adjustments for deferred maintenance are common to all real estate appraisals and should always be considered in the appraisal of golf projects.

3. The greens fee multiplier was first described by Lawrence A. Hirsh, MAI, in "Golf Courses – Valuation and Evaluation," *The Appraisal Journal* (January 1991), 38–47.

Functional problems in golf facilities can also explain price differences between properties. Excessive or penal fairway layouts and hazards that are very difficult for the casual golfer may cause a facility to lose business from this market segment. The appraiser can account for factors of this type with an adjustment in annual rounds.

Operating cost differences between golf courses may be revealed by studying their financial statements. These differences can explain why golf course prices vary significantly when other circumstances indicate that they should not. High operating costs may be attributed to inept management, which is a curable item, or to more serious factors such as the quantity and quality of the water supply or an inefficient course layout that results in excessive maintenance expenses.

Any number of items can account for differences between golf courses. The appraiser should look for major items that can be explained and quantified; it is fruitless to try to account for everything. Construction of a market data grid may facilitate the visual presentation of data and the analytical process. A sample golf course sales analysis is shown in Figure 9.3.

FIGURE 9.3 GOLF COURSE SALES ANALYSIS

	Subject	Sale 1	Sale 2	Sale 3
Physical Characteristics				
No. of holes	18	18	18	18
Clubhouse (sq. ft.)	5,500	4,200	8,100	5,800
Practice greens	Yes	Yes	Yes	No
Driving range	Yes	Yes	Yes	No
Car storage	Good	Average	Excellent	Good
Course rating*	35 (Good)	32 (Avg.)	39 (Good)	27 (Avg.)
Food & beverage	Average	Average	Excellent	Good
Condition	Average	Average	Good	Good
Other amenities†	L,R,B,T	L,R	L,R,B,S	B,T,S
Financial Data				
Price		$4,370,000	$5,600,000	$3,400,000
Date	11/90	11/89	8/89	11/88
Rounds	38,000	44,000	52,000	29,000
Total revenue	$1,350,000	$1,560,000	$1,610,000	$1,405,000
Golf revenue	$1,001,000	$940,000	$1,240,000	$780,000
Avg. greens fee	$25.02	$20.36	$21.38	$23.90
Value Indicators				
Total revenue multiplier (*TRM*)	3.25 (est.)	2.80	3.48	2.42
Golf revenue multiplier (*GRM*)	4.50 (est.)	4.65	4.52	4.36
Price per round (*PPR*)	$115.00 (est.)	$99.32	$107.69	$117.24
Greens fee and rounds multiplier (*GFM*)	4.90 (est.)	4.88	5.04	4.91

*From golf course rating data (See Chapter 2.)
†L=lockers, R=rain shelters, B=bag storage, T=tennis courts, S=swimming pool
Note: Value indicators (multipliers) for the subject property were estimated and used to derive a range of value estimates.

By total revenue multiplier (*TRM*): 3.25 × $1,350,000 = $4,387,500
By golf revenue multiplier (*GRM*): 4.50 × $1,001,000 = $4,504,500
By price per round (*PPR*): $115 × 38,000 = $4,370,000
By greens fee and rounds multiplier (*GFM*): 4.90 × $25.02 × 38,000 = $4,658,724
Conclusion: A value range of $4,400,000 to $4,650,000 is indicated.

In many appraisal assignments the real estate must be separated from the non-real estate components of the property. This situation arises in valuations for lending purposes where the real property alone represents the security for the loan. The cost approach can be employed to derive a separate value estimate for the FF&E and the business component can be quantified using the techniques described in Chapter 7 or by comparative analyses.

In valuation assignments where it is necessary to separate the physical assets (i.e., real estate and FF&E) from the intangible aspects or business value of a golf facility, another step must be added to the analytical process.

VALUING THE BUSINESS COMPONENT

If properly applied, the sales comparison approach can provide an automatic allowance for the intangible assets of the golf facility being appraised. A separate value estimate or adjustment for this factor such as is made in the cost approach is often unnecessary. However, separate consideration is necessary in some cases; when the comparable sales represent under performing golf courses; when the transactions were made under duress and only the existing facilities were considered; and when the transactions involved sales of property subject to an operating lease. Such factors will be revealed in the investigative process. Needless to say, the analyst must understand the typical aspects of a real estate transaction and the unique considerations involved in the sale of a business.

It is generally beyond the scope of a golf course appraisal assignment to appraise a comparable sale property, except in extraordinary circumstances. It is proper for appraisers to allocate a sale price as do buyers, sellers, and their representatives, as long as a realistic value is placed on the components of the total assets involved in a transaction.

If the appraiser only applies the sales comparison and income approaches to value and the assignment requires segregation of the various value components, a distinct and separate analysis must be conducted to appraise the business. This work can be another aspect of the sales comparison approach, or a distinct process, as described in Chapter 7.

Golf course business opportunities exist when facilities are leased, typically by municipalities, to operators. Sales of leaseholds usually involve the personal property or FF&E and the intangible assets or business enterprise, but they may also include interests in improvements made to the golf course or clubhouse by the lessee.

The following example illustrates the financial aspects of such a transaction and important analytical data that can be useful to the appraiser. Consider a local municipal course subject to a 25-year lease. It was leased five years ago by an experienced golf pro who improved the greens and fairways, renovated the clubhouse, added new cars, and vastly upgraded the image of the facility. The rent schedule has a guaranteed step-up clause and includes a percentage formula that allows the lessee to recapture his investment in the improvements and the lessor to share in the success of the operation.

The golf course produces a net income of $425,000 after management compensation, but before rent payments of $250,000; the golf pro just sold his leasehold for $1,000,000. Investigation of this sale reveals that the price was allocated as follows: $420,000 to the FF&E and $580,000 to intangibles such as the license to operate, favorable contracts, the business systems in place, a short-term management contract, and golfer lists.

A nearby golf course with similar characteristics, but no lease, was sold for $3,500,000. Assuming that this figure represents the approximate value of the subject course, the two transactions indicate an allocation of $2,500,000 for the land and golf course improvements, $420,000 for FF&E, and $580,000 for the intangibles of the enterprise, which are sometimes inaccurately referred to as *goodwill*. The capitalization rates are 12.1% for the overall property ($425,000/$3,500,000), 17.5% for the business ($175,000/$1,000,000), and 10% for the real property ($250,000/$2,500,000).

With this type of information and other statistics from the operating statement of the comparable golf course, comparative techniques can be used to appraise the business component of a going concern separately. In a successful course, the intangible component of the total enterprise can be quite significant. In the example described, the intangibles amounted to about one-sixth of the value of the golf course operation. Unlike sales of retail or service businesses, transactions involving the sale of golf course leaseholds as business opportunities are quite rare. Specialists in the field should keep a careful record of these sales when they do occur.

MIXED USES

A golf course or country club appraisal assignments can sometimes involve a combination of other land uses held in one ownership or security interest. For example, a resort and recreational golf facility may be combined with surrounding single-family home and condominium developments in a master project.

In the application of the sales comparison approach, the other land uses can be separately valued with comparative techniques using appropriate multipliers and unit value indicators. The sum of the parts can produce an indication of the total project value when consideration is given to the risk, appropriate returns, and yield requirements associated with mixed-use projects. Appraisers involved in such assignments should be familiar with the techniques employed in the valuation of lodging, racquet sport, health and fitness, restaurant, and retail facilities.

CHAPTER TEN

SPECIAL VALUATION PROBLEMS

 Most golf course appraisal assignments are performed to assist clients with buying, selling, or financing. A market study is a typical adjunct to the analytical process. However, there are many atypical situations in which a golf course appraiser may be asked to render valuation or consultation services.

VALUATION OF A NONPROFIT COURSE

Private clubs can present unusual analytical problems. The appraiser should recognize that the nonprofit aspect of the club is limited to its financial operations, not its amenities. The club should not necessarily be penalized in terms of value because the bottom line does not look good. Financial statements may not give a true picture of the income-producing potential of the property and they do not reflect the value contribution of club amenities.

On a theoretical basis, the value of a private club can be compared to the recognized status of a private residence. In both cases, the financial return is in the form of amenities. A nonprofit club has value to its members because it yields social, recreational, and cultural benefits rather than a net income stream. The appraiser must find a way to quantify these subjective amenities or find a substitute rationale that will adequately support the value conclusion.

The purpose of the appraisal assignment has a direct bearing on the valuation approaches to be used and how much weight should be given to each. For financing purposes it is critical that the club be able to support debt service after an allowance is made for adequate reserves. If a valuation is required for assessment purposes, the procedures to be followed and the factors to be considered may vary from one state to another. Because the purpose of the appraisal will determine how the nonprofit club is to be analyzed, the following discussion relates to the application of the three approaches to value under various circumstances.

Cost Approach

The cost approach should always be applied in appraising a nonprofit golf facility. The assets to be included and the depreciation to be estimated will vary depending on the assignment.

In any appraisal, except when the golf club is being sold for redevelopment, land value should be based on sales or other data indicating the value of raw land designated or suitable for golf course use. The transactions analyzed should be limited to those involving land sold for exclusive golf course use that has a highest and best use for development as a golf course in the foreseeable future. Where there is a paucity of these sales, it may be possible to extract a value indicator for raw golf course land from a transaction that involved a combination of residential and recreational land use in a master-planned community.

Certain assets or cost factors that might normally be thought to contribute to the value of a golf facility will normally be excluded from consideration. The value of intangible assets such as reputation, name, and course design would not be considered unless the purpose of the appraisal was to determine value in exchange. For ad valorem tax purposes, any valuation consideration relating to the business enterprise should be excluded. Moreover, an allowance for entrepreneurial profit is rarely included.

All categories of depreciation should be analyzed and applied, but no deduction should be attributed to the nonprofit status of the property. External obsolescence due to the lack of operating profits is not to be considered if profits are not generated by choice; this fact may be considered when demographic changes in the market area have undermined the membership status of the facility and its ability to generate sufficient revenues to meet normal operating costs.

Income Approach

Capitalizing the income stream of an entity that is not supposed to produce profits may be questionable. However, the term *nonprofit* does not necessarily mean that the golf club cannot realize a net income. Court decisions have interpreted the term to apply to operations that produce net income to be used for organizational purposes such as making improvements and meeting debt service, but not for making a profit. Depending on the purpose of the assignment, the appraiser may impute to the subject, nonprofit facility an income stream based upon the operating results of similar clubs that are operated to produce a profit and are put to their highest and best use.

In estimating revenue the appraiser should employ normal comparative techniques and make adjustments for differences in dues, greens fees, and other income sources such as driving range fees, pro shop sales, and food and beverage sales. Initiation fees and related transfer fees of nonproprietary memberships may or may not be considered depending upon the revenue categories and characteristics of the golf facilities used as comparables. Obviously the research required to value a nonprofit club is more complicated than the research required in an appraisal assignment involving a similar, profit-oriented club.

Just as an appraiser may impute a market-driven fee schedule, the number of golf rounds may be adjusted. A nonprofit facility may not maximize its operating capacity because of a stated policy or limitations on the number of golf memberships. Operating expenses should be treated in a similar manner. Many people believe that private clubs have inefficient management. This is not always true, but in approaching this part of the analysis the appraiser should expect to find excessive operating costs or underutilization of facilities. A detailed study of each expense category may be justified.

The income approach should be thoroughly explored, but applied with extreme caution. It is the one approach always available to the appraiser; there may or may not be sufficient sales of profit-oriented golf courses to employ the sales comparison approach.

Sales Comparison Approach

As a general rule, sales of profit-oriented golf courses or clubs should not be considered in valuing a nonprofit course if their prices include an allowance for a highest and best use unrelated to the sport or business of golf. A sale of a nonprofit golf course can be considered provided the land is permanently dedicated to golf use. In any case substantial research is involved in the analysis of golf course transactions. The analyst must bear in mind that enormous efforts are made by golf course developers and architects to make each course distinctive; therefore, comparisons can be quite complicated. The demographics of each course's market area should be examined and appropriate adjustments should be made where indicated. An appraisal handbook dealing with nonprofit courses lists the following items that should be considered in making comparisons; most of these items are also applicable to profit-oriented facilities:[1]

1. *Location*
   Distance from playing populace
   Interrelationship with subdivision
   Access and parking
2. *Climate*
   Length of playing season
   Wind direction and velocity
   Frequency of play-stopping storms
3. *Playability*
   Course challenge
      Player appeal
      Steep fairways
      Aesthetic design
      Surface drainage
      Size of greens
      Width of fairways
      Shrub and tree maturity
   Course condition
4. *Irrigation system*
   Reliable water source
   Water cost (pumping costs or vendor charges)
   Water quality
   System type (fully automatic, etc.)
   Other (treated effluent, water rights, etc.)
5. *Soil type and texture*
   Intrinsic drainage, water-holding capacity
   Salinity or alkalinity
6. *Tools, equipment, and rental items*
   Type
   Condition
   Income produced (golf cars, carts, clubs, etc.)
7. *Practice range*
8. *Size*
   Acreage
   Number of holes
9. *Improvements—size and condition*
   Clubhouse
      Bar
      Restaurant
      Clubroom
      Locker rooms
   Pro shop

1. California State Board of Equalization Assessors' Handbook, *The Appraisal of Golf Courses*, April 1971, revised September 1975.

Pool
Tennis courts
10. *Financial factors*
Outstanding debt
Number of members
Monthly dues
Minimum to be spent at bar or restaurant
Greens fees
History of special assessments
Annual operating costs
Rounds played annually
11. *Sales terms and conditions*
Sale price
Trust deeds or mortgages including chattels
Interest rates
Terms of loans
Leases (especially leaseback)
Options
Mineral rights
Liquor license included in sale price or financing

Stock and Debt Approach

A private, nonprofit club may be publicly held with stock that is traded on a formal or informal basis. The stock represents the equity in the property, and the current price applied to the number of shares added to the outstanding debt could provide an indication of the total value of the golf facility. Where the sale of memberships is handled by club management, the appraiser should ascertain whether the share price is set by the open market or administered in some fashion to control the price. Also, when the eligibility of buyers is based on select criteria that limit the number of purchasers, the share price may not be indicative of fair market value.

The stock debt approach should not be the only approach applied in the appraisal of a nonprofit club because there are too many potential valuation problems and adjustments that must be considered. For example, an appraiser might need to consider whether the number of memberships is appropriate; most clubs favor a range of 400 to 600. Other variables that could adversely affect share pricing are the amount of monthly dues and future special assessments.

Selecting an Approach

Nonprofit golf facilities and country clubs are difficult to appraise. Moreover, their special tax status may be in jeopardy due to charges of discriminatory practices. The best indicators of value are data from sales of similar private clubs, but the adjustment process is complicated. The income approach is preferred when sales of clubs are limited or include special consideration for other highest and best uses of the land. The cost approach is quite complicated, but can be useful as a check on the other two approaches. An allowance for the business component of the investment is appropriate and can represent a substantial sum when the course has a prestigious reputation and there is a waiting list for new members. All of the market analysis and valuation techniques appropriate to profit-oriented clubs should be considered in appraising a nonprofit golf facility.

◄
Pebble Beach Golf
Links is a world-
class facility.

VALUATION OF A TROPHY PROPERTY

Trophy properties have the very best construction quality and are generally thought of as world-class in both reputation and location. A trophy golf course is characterized by a "signature" architect, exceptional design and layout, a one-of-a-kind location, and high fees. Pebble Beach Golf Links in California is a good example of a trophy golf course.

Since 1985 foreign buyers, notably Japanese investors, have been making well-publicized purchases of golf properties in select locations in Hawaii and the continental United States. The prices paid have astounded the public and motivated many owners to sell their properties when they would not otherwise have been so inclined. Prices of more than $100 million have been paid for 18-hole championship courses with excellent supporting amenities.

Normal financial considerations do not support these prices, which indicate capitalization rates as low as 2.5%. Does this mean that there is a two-tier pricing structure for certain existing courses? What is their market value if these special acquisitions cannot be predicted? Will this acquisition program continue in the future and affect other parts of the United States?

These and many other questions have been asked and will continue to be asked by owners, developers, brokers, consultants, and others. Many seminars and conferences have been devoted to this subject. It may not be possible to provide satisfactory responses to these concerns at this time. However, examining some of the forces that have propelled this phenomenon will reveal partial answers and may assist in understanding the investors' rationale.

In Japan there is an extreme shortage of developable land and unit prices are exorbitant by U.S. standards. A recent article revealed that suburban office building sites in Japan have exceeded $1,200 per square foot and downtown locations have reached a high of $23,500 per square foot.[2] Japanese businessmen were reportedly accustomed to paying as much as $500

2. "Office Rates: Japan vs. the United States," *Appraisal Views*, vol. 2, no. 4.

for a round of golf and up to $1,000,000 for memberships in exclusive, private clubs. The game has become extremely popular, compelling entrepreneurs to search out alternative locations to meet the demands of the golfing public.

The first target for investment was Hawaii, which is a very popular vacation spot among the Japanese. Eight courses were acquired there between 1986 and 1990. Actual golf course prices are difficult to ascertain, because many acquisitions involved multi-faceted resorts, but the general range was $50 million and up. When this source of supply was depleted, attention focused on the territory of Guam, which is a favorite vacation destination for average Japanese wage earners, and the states of California, South Carolina, and Florida. Prior to the preparation of this book, there have been more than 50 acquisitions or development proposals in these four locations at prices that would have been unheard of a few years ago. It has recently been reported that Japanese investors are now turning their attention to locations in Texas and around the metropolitan areas of Portland, Seattle, Chicago, and Atlanta. The trend is likely to shift in emphasis from acquisitions of existing golf facilities to the development of new, mixed-use projects. In these projects golf courses will be combined with upscale residential subdivisions that target international executives and resorts with a wide range of amenities that appeal to high-income families.

The trend of paying prices that are at least twice as high as those indicated by normal investment criteria is not likely to continue indefinitely. Many Japanese acquisitions prior to 1990 were fueled by borrowed capital at interest rates as low as 3%. The equivalent cost of capital in Japan is now in the 7% range, which is still highly favorable by U.S. standards. Furthermore, investor equity positions have been severely eroded by the huge stock market decline in Japan.

A second factor that motivated Japanese investors and trading companies to acquire golf properties at high prices was the ability to sell very high-priced memberships to Japanese businessmen and other foreign executives who are golf enthusiasts. Obviously if memberships in exclusive country clubs or private golf facilities are sold at prices of $500,000 or more, it is fairly easy to recapture a substantial amount of investment capital. However, the market segment expected to account for such memberships has declined because of the fall of the Nikkei index, economic uncertainties associated with crises throughout the world, and sluggish financial conditions. In addition, complaints about the overselling of memberships in Japan have been well publicized. Some golfers have paid $100,000 to $250,000 for memberships and still have to endure long lines at courses and driving ranges.

All of these factors tend to indicate that the unusually high prices paid for trophy and signature golf courses in the best locations will not likely be achieved again. However, prices for other golf properties will most likely stay at levels that are supported by basic economic factors.

VALUATION FOR EMINENT DOMAIN

All three approaches can be employed in the usual manner to appraise the whole property in a condemnation assignment. There is nothing unique to be considered in the valuation of a full taking; partial takings of golf courses, however, are another matter.

A common problem in eminent domain actions involving golf courses is the taking of land that represents part or all of one or more fairways or greens. In these cases substantial expertise is needed to analyze the effect of the taking on the remainder and the probable costs to cure part or all of the problem. A substantial allowance for severance damage can usually be expected.

In some golf course takings it may be possible to relocate the lost holes on the remaining land area. This means that the course must be rerouted, and major costs will be incurred to reconfigure the irrigation system, realign the existing holes affected by the new layout, design and build new holes, relocate the car paths, and prepare the membership to deal with construction inconveniences. Even after all this is done, the golf course may be less desirable to players and be diminished in value. As part of the analytical process, the appraiser should consult the golf course superintendent, golf course architects and builders, the manager of the facility, and representatives of the membership.

If, in a partial taking, replacement of the lost holes is impossible or impractical, it may be necessary to downsize the entire course, making it a par-3 executive-type course or converting the remaining land to a short course of nine holes. Under these circumstances the negative impact on memberships would be enormous and change the financial aspects of the operations. If fewer rounds are available to the club membership and outside golfers, fewer cars and less clubhouse area would be required due to the reduced number of golfers, and many aspects of the operation would be affected. At the same time, there could be excess land available for disposal as a result of the downsizing process. Only a highly experienced golf course appraiser should attempt to deal with such a complicated appraisal problem.

Another possibility in a partial taking is that the remaining golf course acreage may no longer be suitable for its designed purpose. This situation requires a highest and best use study, an appraisal of the land for an alternative use, and consideration of the salvage value of the clubhouse or other buildings. Public authorities responsible for determining right-of-way alignments or boundary lines for other types of takings should be made aware of the extensive impact a partial taking has on a golf course. The responsible agency exposes itself to a potential claim for substantial severance damages.

VALUATION FOR TAX ASSESSMENT

States may have unique rules for appraising golf courses for real property taxation purposes. The appraiser should be familiar with all applicable statutes before undertaking the assignment. Special rules or case law may also affect the procedures involved in the valuation of nonprofit facilities and country clubs. The appraiser should segregate the total value of the facility into real property taxable elements (e.g., land, golf course, improvements, buildings, parking lot), personal property elements (e.g., furniture, fixtures, equipment, rolling stocks, inventory), and intangibles.

Appraisers must recognize that the income and sales comparison approaches can automatically provide an allowance for the value of the business enterprise component in a golf course and that this factor is not subject to assessment or taxation.

VALUATION OF A LEASEHOLD

Often golf courses are leased by an operating entity, which results in the creation of an owner's interest (the leased fee) and a tenant's interest (the leasehold estate). The appraiser may be asked to appraise either or all of the interests. The value of the leased fee is represented by the sum of the net present value (*NPV*) of the future rent payments plus the reversionary interest, or remainder value, of the golf course when the lease is terminated. The value of the leasehold is represented by the *NPV* of the tenant's operating income over the term of the lease.

Because the tenant is operating a business, net income is attributed to 1) the difference between economic rent and contract rent and 2) the income received in excess of economic rent. The value attributed to a leasehold can vary greatly depending on the status of the property at the start of the lease, the capital investment in the golf course made by the lessee, and other terms of the lease transaction. Many golf courses originate with a lease of raw land; all necessary improvements are developed by the lessee. Leases involving existing courses may require only a small amount of upgrading by the tenant. In addition to any leasehold interest in the real property resulting from the lease agreement, the tenant typically provides the personal property and investment capital necessary to operate the course.

A step-by-step process for allocating the net operating income of a leased golf course can be illustrated with the following calculations:

A. *NOI* (stabilized) of golf course	$640,000
B. Less contract rental payment to lessor	$300,000
C. *NOI* attributed to leasehold and business (A minus B)	$340,000
D. Economic rent (based on appraisal)	$450,000
E. *NOI* attributed to leasehold (D minus B)	$150,000
F. *NOI* attributed to business (C minus E)	$190,000
G. *NOI* attributed to return on and recapture of investment in operating capital, personal property and inventory (See example in Chapter 7.)	$120,000
H. *NOI* attributed to intangible assets (F minus G)	$70,000

In the above example the total value of the business enterprise is the *NPV* of the *NOI* attributed to the leasehold (E) over the remaining term of the lease, plus the market value of the personal property, plus the *NPV* of the *NOI* attributed to intangible assets (H).

One of the most difficult tasks in the appraisal of a leased interest in a golf course is obtaining current data on rental rates or lease terms for comparative purposes. The best sources of lease rental data are parks and recreation departments or representatives of local, government agencies. A typical lease will provide for a guaranteed rent plus a percentage rent. The minimum portion generally provides for a fixed return on the value of the property being leased, while the percentage portion allows the lessor to share in property appreciation, gain protection from inflation, and share in any excess business profits. In most percentage lease clauses, different percentage rates are applied to different sources of revenue. For example, it is common to find percentage rates of up to 25% applied to golf revenues and rates of 5% applied to food and beverage, pro shop, and concession sales.

The expected future performance of a leased golf facility may result in an irregular, but increasing, projected net income and rental income stream. Under these conditions, the appraiser must use a discounted cash flow (DCF) analysis to make an accurate estimate of value, whether the assignment is to value the owner's or tenant's interest. The number of years employed in the projection should be limited to the future point in time when the golf course operations become relatively stabilized. After stabilization future increases in revenue will be closely linked to changes in the consumer price index or some other type of index that measures growth or financial expectations in the business of golf.

Appraisers are cautioned not to try to appraise a tenant's interest in a golf facility without obtaining appropriate market data to support an estimate of the economic rental value of the leased property. The total value of the leasehold interest may be correctly estimated, but a review appraiser may have reason to reject the report if the rental value estimate is unsupported.

The capitalization rates applied in the valuation of a leasehold can be multiple in character and will differ from the rates applied to a fee simple interest in a golf facility. The yield curve shown in Figure 10.1 illustrates how yields for various property interests can vary in golf course valuation.

FIGURE 10.1 CAPITALIZATION RATE VARIANCE

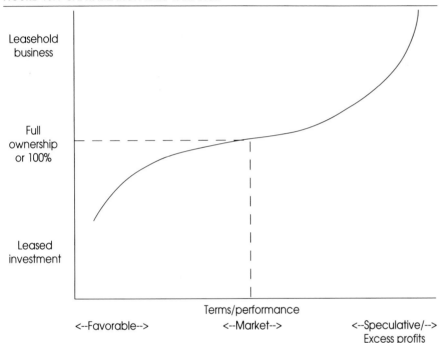

For example, the following capitalization rates could be considered applicable in the appraisal of a leased golf course in which all of the interests are to be identified and quantified:

Owner's interest in guaranteed rent	9%-11%
Owner's interest in percentage rent	12%-14%
Full fee simple interest in entire operation	12%-14%
Leasehold interest in excess of actual or economic rent over contract rent	14%-16%
Excess profits attributed to returns over and above investment requirements of operating capital	20%-25%

Readers are cautioned not to adopt these rates, but rather to conduct appropriate research to identify the current yields expected to be received by informed investors and golf course operators. At some point in the future, the Appraisal Institute or National Golf Foundation may conduct research and publish the results of a survey of golf course investors. Until that time, golf course appraisers, analysts, and investors will have to perform traditional investigations questioning participants in recent transactions.

VALUATION FOR PRICE SEGREGATION

Price segregation appraisals allow buyers of golf facilities to reduce their income taxes by enhancing depreciation deductions.[3] Prior to the implementation of the Tax Reform Act of 1986, real estate investors obtained purchase price allocation and remaining life studies to increase depreciation deductions and segregate the cost of property eligible for investment tax credits. Although these tax credits have been eliminated, the new Modified Accelerated Cost Recovery System (MACRS) still provides shorter depreciable lives for personal property and certain categories of improvements.

Depreciation Benefits

Most real property falls into one of two class life classifications: 27.5 year residential or 31.5 year nonresidential. Land improvements generally qualify for 15 years; the personal property associated with commercial real estate has a class life of five or seven years.

To maximize depreciation deductions, three methods of depreciation are applied to the various property class lives. Assets with lives of 10 years or less may be depreciated by the 200% declining balance (DDB) method. Assets with 10- to 20-year lives may be depreciated with the 150% declining balance (150 DB) method. Finally, real property with class lives of 27.5 and 31.5 years is limited to the straight-line (SL) method.

To maximize depreciation deductions, the taxpayer must obtain a price segregation appraisal that: 1) allocates a separate value to the land portion of investment, and 2) determines which parts of the remaining physical assets fall into the special categories eligible for faster depreciation (both shorter lives and accelerated methods).

Because the 1986 laws lengthened depreciable lives on the whole, it is imperative to identify the shortest period over which each asset category can be depreciated.

Identifying Short-Lived Assets

To qualify for faster depreciation under MACRS, an asset generally must be "tangible personal property" and it must not be a "structural component." The courts have concluded that permanency is the best indication that an asset is a structural component, not personal property. Six questions are posed to help taxpayers and their representatives determine permanency.

- Is the property capable of being moved, and has it in fact been moved?
- Is the property designed or constructed to remain permanently in place?
- Are there circumstances that tend to show the expected or intended length of affixation?
- How substantial a job is removal of the property, and how time-consuming is it?
- How much damage will the property sustain upon removal of the property?
- What is the manner of affixation of the property to the land?

Improvement Components With Short Lives

The definition of *structural component* is broad, but certain types of assets constitute personal property.

Computer support installations needed to house computers qualify for

3. Robert M. Hersh and Jerry S. Williford, "The Tax Advantages of Cost Segregation Studies," *Real Estate Review*, vol. 20, no. 2 (Summer 1990), 63–68.

a five-year life. Such construction may include raised floors that cover the wiring, special electrical systems installed to operate the computers, and special air-conditioning and humidity-control systems required to maintain the computers.

Security and decorative lighting, which is commonly found in commercial buildings, is considered to be personal property, not a structural component.

Many items found in company kitchens also qualify as personal property. Built-in cabinets have been found to be personal property. Also included in this category are movable file systems, carpets, drapes, blinds, computers that regulate and control the building's lighting, heating and air-conditioning systems, pneumatic tube systems, fire extinguishers, and similar items.

Generally, all of the items listed above can be depreciated over five to seven years using the DDB method.

In addition to the personal property inside a building, some land improvements qualify for shorter lives and an accelerated method of depreciation. Many golf course land improvements can be depreciated over 15 years using the 150 DB method. These land improvements include

- Sidewalks
- Drainage systems
- Parking lots
- Landscaping, greens, fairways, etc.
- Roads and paths
- Sewers
- Fencing
- Outside lighting

The IRS treats all improvements to land (other than buildings), whether they are improvements to real or personal property, as land improvements.

Golf Course Segregation Study

The information shown in Figure 10.2 pertains to a golf course acquired at a cost of $18,200,000. This course produces first-year depreciation of $589,588 and second-year depreciation of $1,007,126, for a total depreciation estimate of $1,596,714. If the owner had not undertaken a price segregation study, the straight-line depreciation applicable to the first two years would have totaled $719,672. At a marginal tax rate of 28%, the investment savings for two years is $245,572.

To prepare a price segregation study like the one depicted in Figure 10.2, the appraiser must first appraise the property or business and determine the land value component, if any. The residual value is attributed to the building(s), land improvements, personal property, and intangible assets and then allocated by applying depreciated replacement cost analysis and other techniques. Any "excess" purchase price should be carefully studied to determine if it is attributable to an intangible value element, which is depreciable, or to business goodwill, which is not.

FIGURE 10.2 GOLF COURSE SEGREGATION STUDY

Asset Category	Allocated Price*	Life (Years)	Depreciation Method	First-Year Depreciation†	Second-Year Depreciation
Land	$6,624,000	0.0	N/A	—	—
Basic structures	3,080,011	31.5	SL‡	$93,704	$97,778
Land improvements	7,598,850	20.0	150DB§	379,943	721,891
Office/restaurant equipment	119,500	10.0	DDB‖	17,071	29,265
Information systems	7,000	6.0	DDB	1,400	2,240
Vehicles	487,350	4.0	DDB	97,470	155,952
Inventory & goodwill	283,289	N/A	—	—	—
Totals, segregated	$18,200,000			$589,588	$1,007,126
Totals, unsegregated	$11,576,000#	31.5	SL	$352,180	$367,492
Depreciation advantage				$237,408	$639,634
Potential tax advantage	(28% rate)**			$66,474	$179,098

* Allocation based on appraisal.
† A convention in the statute allows for only a partial-year deduction in the first year. Thus, for office/restaurant equipment, the first-year calculation is: $119,500 ÷ 7 = $17,071 × 2.0 = $34,142 ÷ 2 = $17,071. A similar methodology is applied to the other asset categories.
‡ Straight-line method; apply mid-month convention in first year.
§ 150% declining balance method; apply mid-year convention in first year.
‖ Double declining balance method; apply mid-year convention in first year.
Calculated by substracting the land value from the total sale price.
** Tax advantage extends beyond two years. For the purpose of this illustration, the example has been limited.

Note: Readers are cautioned to consult a tax expert before relying on the methodology described here. This example assumes the golf course was acquired on the first day of the year.

Chapter Eleven

FINANCING A GOLF PROJECT

 The extraordinary popularity of golf as an investment as well as entertainment has spurred unusual activity in golf course development, acquisition, and brokerage. Entire publications are devoted to the subject, reporting on recent sales, proposals for construction, marketing results, contacts in the field, debt and equity financing, and current products.[1] Seminars on golf course-related issues have been drawing large audiences from coast to coast.

Most of the current interest in golf among business people pertains to real estate loans, development opportunities, profit maximization, management ideas, and the marketing of courses. Financing considerations are of prime importance because the ability to borrow funds will be the major determinant of future golf course development and transactions.

Unfortunately, the current mortgage financing situation is not good due to the savings and loan debacle of the 1980s and the national budget deficit and debt crisis. Many lenders see golf course properties as too specialized and risky, and beyond their evaluation capabilities. At this time most financial institutions are not anxious to make loans for recreational projects.

The limitations of financial markets are of great significance to the golf industry. The timing of the economic decline is especially bad because the golf industry has been primed to expand to serve the vast increase in demand expected to take place in the next decade. The industry must address this problem so that possible solutions can be identified.

Some golf projects will always be able to attract mortgage financing, but many well-planned projects may not get started due to the lack of debt funding. Successful owners, developers, and project managers must know how to maximize their real estate financing capabilities in the early stages of transactions to avoid failure. The guidelines presented here can assist potential borrowers. Current lending procedures for the golf industry are described and ways to improve these practices are explored.

INVESTMENT CHARACTERISTICS

Golf is a business first and a real estate investment second. This is the perception of the industry. The unique characteristics and complexity of golf investments affect their financing capabilities. Most golf facilities comprise a number of business activities operating under a single management entity. This fact alone can give a golf loan a negative rating because the lender may not have the capability to evaluate various levels of management. Furthermore, key individuals may not remain with a project throughout the term of a loan.

A golf facility is a special-purpose property. It may be a single-purpose property if it has no future potential for conversion to an alternative use.

1. See the publications listed in the bibliography.

This can be seen as a big disadvantage to lenders. As a general rule, single- or special-purpose properties are considered as anathema to good lending practice. Rather than deal with the problem by applying unusual or stringent standards and mortgage terms, lenders typically adopt a policy of providing no loans whatsoever.

Fortunately, golf courses do not have the negative image associated by some other, consumer-oriented recreational properties. The golf industry has not had a problem with consumer complaints, misleading advertising, bankruptcies, and unprofessional management. Industry problems generally relate to environmental issues; discrimination cases, which can materially affect income tax status; assessments for taxation; and a lack of affordable land.

One curable problem is the lack of standardized financial statements and comparative statistics for golf facilities. The hospitality, or lodging, industry recognized this problem many years ago and has promoted the industry-wide use of standardized revenue and expense statements and operating statistics. By gathering, organizing, and publishing operating statistics from a wide range of hotels, motels, and resorts, the lodging industry has enhanced the knowledge of the business, making it easier for appraisers to analyze the results of individual properties and judge their performance. In the golf industry, this kind of data is lacking, except for limited operating statistics for country clubs. The Professional Golfers' Association and the National Golf Foundation have recognized the problem and are planning to take a bigger role in gathering and reporting information in the future.

Golf courses are more land-intensive than any other real estate use. Many will agree that this use of land is inefficient. A lack of large, developable sites and increasing land prices will prevent many projects from being conceived. The only possible solutions to this problem are utilizing outlying parcels for golf course development and encouraging local governments to promote the use of open space, excess land, undeveloped or paper subdivisions, and unused park property for golf. Rezoning land designated for open space or another protected use for golf course or country club development is politically explosive in most communities. This is not a likely scenario, even when the promoter offers to pay huge sums for the legal entitlements. Thus, only golf projects planned for small communities or new towns in outlying locations are most likely to have affordable land prices. Whether these projects are financially feasible is a completely separate subject.

After the problem of finding a golf course site has been solved, water is the most critical development factor. The current availability of water and the guarantee of an adequate future supply is crucial in the decision-making process. In arid areas where there is concern and emotional debate about the adequacy of future water supplies, golf courses are being blamed, rightfully or not, for declines in the ground water table. Such a situation can result in restrictions on the irrigation of fairways.

Lenders are not overly concerned about the tax-shelter characteristics of golf courses, unless they have an ownership interest. Golf courses have never been considered good tax shelters; they are too land-intensive. This used to mean that golf projects were not attractive vehicles for raising capital through syndications. Now that current tax laws have discouraged syndications, golf projects are no worse off than other real estate investments. In fact the shorter lives attributed to land improvements, machinery, and other personal property can make a golf investment competitive in terms of depreciation deductions with other real estate investments that have a smaller land value component. (See Chapter 10.)

This discussion of the investment characteristics of golf courses is not exhaustive and does not specifically identify negative investment or financing considerations. Projects are being funded on a selective basis. A survey of lenders was conducted in the summer of 1990 to provide information of assistance to future borrowers. The complete survey and the responses recorded can be found at the end of this text.

LENDING PRACTICES

Institutional financing for golf projects cannot be discussed with certainty because the available data are extremely limited and systematic surveys or research studies are rare. Although golf courses have been financed by institutions for many decades, their track record has not been documented. There is no reason to believe that their overall historical performance has been poor, but projects have been ill-conceived and are obvious candidates for failure.

Most golf projects have been financed by commercial banks, savings and loan institutions, and other sources such as investment bankers, mortgage bankers and brokers, and credit corporations. In today's market only a small percentage of these institutions are in the market for golf project loans. Some of the most active lenders are nontraditional sources such as investment arms of public and private firms and credit corporations. Greyhound Financial Corporation, GATX Golf Capital, U.S. Golf Investment Company, G.E. Capital, and USF&G Realty have all made golf loans. Most lenders are large with total assets ranging from $500 million to more than $25 billion. They prefer projects with 18-hole, regulation courses, but they will consider public, private, or resort-oriented courses as long as they are supported by strong economics. Loans for development financing for construction, refinancing, and expansion or renovation are preferred over initial take-out financing upon completion of construction and bridge financing for acquisitions.

The mortgage terms that lenders offer to golf project borrowers vary greatly. Loans are generally short term, of five years or less, and are partially amortizing, typically over 25 years, with a balloon payment. Loans are usually made for, and secured by, the real property, but a pledge of the personal property may be required. Loan-to-value ratios are about the same as those applicable to commercial investment property, ranging from 50% to 80%; debt service coverage ratios range from 1.1 to 1.25. Interest rates, however, are higher than typical, reaching 250 basis points over the prime interest rate. Construction loans will carry a slightly higher rate. Loan-to-cost ratios are more traditional, generally extending between 60% and 90% of the total cost of collateral.

Golf project loans are not available to those with modest financial statements no matter how good the project is. Lenders expect the borrower to have a net worth of from one to five times the amount of the loan. The ratios and criteria used for evaluating loan applications can be ranked in order of importance: 1) debt service coverage ratio; 2) loan-to-cost ratio; 3) loan-to-value ratio; 4) market share as a percentage of the total market; 5) pro forma current ratio after commencement of operations; 6) pro forma quick ratio after commencement of operations; and 7) other factors such as the credit of the sponsor, other profit center potentials, and the quality, experience, and track record of management. Lenders will usually not consider loans under $1 million or over $25 million.

A good track record in golf course and clubhouse management can significantly improve a borrower's ability to obtain financing; the lender may not require outside, professional management. When a golf is part of a mixed-use project, lenders prefer courses combined with single-family homesites or a combination of a residential subdivision and resort. As a percentage of the total project value, the golf course component can vary widely; an acceptable range is 20% to 70%.

Golf project lenders are also concerned with acceptable equity financing. Some lenders will require net income or cash flow participation as a condition of financing. Others will allow the land to be ground leased, generally if the rent is subordinated to the mortgage payments. A sale-leaseback arrangement is another creative possibility. Limited partnerships have been used to raise the seed capital.

Lenders who are active in the market recognize that golf-related facilities can be profitable to their institutions primarily because the number of players is growing and the ratio of demand to supply is favorable. They are very aware of the continued interest of foreign investors and the positive outlook for projects that are well conceived, managed, and positioned. They prefer projects that are associated with a recognized designer or architect.

APPRAISAL REPORT CONSIDERATIONS

Appraising golf courses in today's market is difficult because of the very factors that have contributed to the well-publicized growth and future potential of the game. Most articles dealing with the economic side of golf have trumpeted its outstanding market potential, the shortage of facilities, and the huge potential profits. The public reads about growing tournament purses, the enormous sums being paid for trophy properties, extremely high greens fees at signature courses, expensive new resort facilities being developed in exotic vacation locations, and the wide variety of new equipment developed through emerging technology.

This raging optimism about the business, combined with a paucity of transactions involving average golf courses, make it very difficult for appraisers to derive price indicators and examine investment factors. Some appraisers have had to extend their search for comparable sales to distant cities and states. When such market conditions exist, the validity of valuation estimates tends to decrease.

Lenders must accept a large part of the responsibility for deficient appraisal reports. They should follow their own regulations and only select appraisers who are truly experienced in the field. Appraisers, in turn, need to learn more about the golfing business, sports and business cycles, the influence of management quality, and the potential impact of high interest rates and tight money conditions. Most individuals specializing in real estate appraisal are not experts on these subjects. The need for new educational programs is obvious.

The following discussion focuses on information required to prepare a fully supported analysis and appraisal for lending purposes.

SUCCESSFUL LOAN PROPOSALS

A golf course loan is not a simple real estate transaction. Many lenders emphasize that a successful golf course loan proposal must be treated like a commercial loan proposal; the emphasis is on cash flow, not the underlying value of the physical assets. Consequently, great weight is given to the income approach, especially the detailed projection of departmental revenues and expenses, which is supported by a statistical analysis of industry-wide ratios and historical figures from the subject and competing golf clubs.

In obtaining a loan for proposed facilities, crucial elements of supporting documentation are the market study, the market feasibility analysis, and conclusions relative to market penetration and potential saturation. Estimates of future revenue are completely dependent on these data. Therefore, these studies should be prepared by highly qualified, experienced analysts who are members of the appraiser's firm or independent research specialists. It is not proper to rely solely on a report prepared by unnamed employees of an accounting firm or information derived from a computer databank. Specific knowledge of the competitive properties should be acquired and applied in determining market share, the rate of absorption or project acceptance, and pricing.

The first step in the loan proposal process is the identification of potential lending institutions. For a golf facility this is a rare event. Unless the borrower has an established banking relationship with the lender, the borrower must be prepared to provide the widest possible range of information in the loan proposal package. A basic collection of analytical information and supporting data cannot be expected to do the job.

The contents of a complete appraisal are described throughout this text. An appraisal prepared to obtain a loan should include

- A description of all of the existing and proposed activities and functions of the facility
- Architectural drawings and a clear description of the quality of the improvements and FF&E
- Photographs of the facility, both internal and external
- Maps that illustrate demographic patterns and show the geographical limits of the primary and secondary markets
- A detailed market feasibility analysis of area supply and demand with supporting data for revenue projections and projected rates of growth or absorption
- An analysis of historical operating data covering a sufficient period to reveal current trends
- Detailed descriptions of competitive facilities along with rate schedules, financial data, and operating statistics

Full documentation and explanation of projected future cash flows is the key to valuation and the amount of present and future loans that can be obtained. Aggressive or unrealistic income, expense, and capital improvement projections are not well-received by lenders.

To complement the cash flow projections in the appraisal, the borrower should provide a business and marketing plan. The borrower should include the resumes of critical staff, a credit history, and a personal guarantee, if available. Audited financial statements should be available, including a balance sheet setting forth the equity position and capital contributions. Other documentation should include a title report and required environmental studies plus planning permits and project approval requirements. The adequacy of existing utilities should be described, especially the future supply and pricing of irrigation water.

The borrower should prepare an oral presentation of the loan request in advance. Rehearsals with accountants, mortgage brokers, and golf course consultants or architects can enhance the presentation. Another good technique is to give the loan officers a personal tour of the subject facility and competitive properties.

Loans for golf projects will be available, but the competition is going to be fierce. Borrowers who are not determined and fully prepared will not succeed. Institutional and nontraditional sources of loans must be explored. The process is expensive and time-consuming, but the potential rewards make it worthwhile.

Owners who are interested in selling existing clubs with no unique attributes should be prepared to consider alternatives to conventional funding such as creative financing or leasing arrangements, secondary loans, lease options, and loans with participation clauses.

Chapter Twelve

ANALYZING GOLF COURSE REAL ESTATE PROJECTS

 In recent years more than 50% of all newly developed golf courses have been integral parts of resort-oriented real estate projects or residential communities. The primary motivation for developing a golf course as part of a project is to enhance the economic performance of a hotel, increase the value and rate of absorption of surrounding lots, or create a unique environment that will enhance the status and financial success of the entire project.

In the past a golf course was often treated as a marketing tool; the developer gave little consideration to its long-term management and fiscal requirements. These golf courses with country club facilities were commonly known as *developer's clubs*. This term connotes a combination of unique problems, most of which pertain to membership relations and the propensity for attracting litigation. With rapid growth in the popularity of golf and recognition of the financial viability of golf projects, golf course investments are not treated so casually and considerable attention has focused on the key issues of course design, membership structure, enhancement of frontage, and maximization of profits.

For golf course consultants, the many issues to be considered depend on the time frame of the development cycle and the purpose of the assignment. The planning stage of a golf community is the ideal time to consider specialized land use design issues and to arrange an equity infrastructure that will emphasize the overall goals of the entire project and avoid unnecessary problems with the membership or the subdivision of adjacent land.

TYPES OF GOLF COURSE COMMUNITIES

Golf course communities, or GCCs, are typically differentiated by the operational category of the course, its size, and its layout. Three common types of communities are

1. Residential subdivisions built along an existing golf course.
2. Residential development around a new, municipal golf course.
3. Prestigious courses developed within a master-planned community.

In the first category the development is small and dense, and the housing tends to be less expensive. These projects will attract first-time home buyers in their late 20s and early 30s and empty nesters who are downsizing their housing needs.[1] GCCs built around public courses usually reflect an arrangement in which the developer builds and dedicates a 9-hole or 18-hole course in return for density and unit mix trade-offs. The advantage for the developer is that management and financial obligations for the course

1. Jeffrey Maza, "Golf and Development – A Profitable Match," *RERC Real Estate Report*, vol. 18, no. 6, 13–16.

▶

Many golf courses
are developed as
part of residential
communities.

are transferred to a third party while the developer retains the rights to
control and develop the surrounding land. The advantage for the community
is that it gains a public course and makes no investment.

Development specialists differ on whether a public golf course should
be used as the centerpiece of a GCC. The main problem with the arrangement is that public courses are crowded and not maintained as well as private facilities. However, the home owners can achieve an acceptable level
of protection through carefully prepared CC&Rs and course operating regulations. The housing around municipal courses will have higher densities
and greater affordability.

It is most typical to think of a GCC as a high-quality residential subdivision overlooking a private country club. These projects are costly endeavors and require considerable expertise. Many are partially semiprivate
in nature so they can provide cash flow to the project in the early stages of
its absorption period.

Other common real estate projects featuring a golf amenity are resorts
and business parks. No matter what type of golf project is being considered,
there are a wide variety of development and economic factors to be considered if the project is to meet its goals. Unfortunately, much of the information provided here has been gained as a result of previous development
mistakes.

GOLF COURSE DESIGN OPTIONS

Considerable research has been done on the sizing and layout of courses to
maximize the value of adjacent real estate. For example, publicity has recently been given to the advantage of "sausage-link" courses—i.e., a single
fairway with returning nines or a single fairway continuous. These courses

FIGURE 12.1 REAL ESTATE VALUE OF SAUSAGE-LINK COURSES

Single-fairway, 18-hole course with returning nines.

Double-fairway, continuous, 18-hole course.

are preferred to core or parallel fairway layouts because of the potential for greater amenity frontage. Figure 12.1 shows how a sausage-link course can theoretically achieve a 275% advantage over a parallel fairway course.

An 18-hole golf course is generally 21,000 feet long. If both sides of each fairway are used for amenity frontage, 40,000 linear feet of amenity frontage is available. Since some fairway paralleling and other less-than-ideal layouts will be necessary, a good course using a sausage-link layout can achieve a 75% efficiency factor and 30,000 linear feet of usable amenity frontage. By contrast, a parallel fairway course with no gerrymandering of the holes will yield only about 20% usable frontage, or 8,000 linear feet.

Assuming a $20,000 sales premium for properties with golf course frontage, the sausage-link course would yield significantly more premium income than the parallel fairway course, no matter what type of housing is developed. Table 12.1 illustrates the financial advantages.

The five basic golf course configurations were described in Chapter 1. (See Figure 1.2.) The development characteristics and benefits of each layout are summarized in Figure 12.2.

The actual acreage required for GCCs varies greatly. The minimum size is about 400 acres (half golf and half residential), but many consider such a project to be only marginally feasible. Larger projects of 800 to 1,500 acres allow the developer to spread the cost of the golf course over a larger number of potential residential units and permit greater flexibility in project phasing. The largest parcels can accommodate projects with courses of 27 holes or more.

TABLE 12.1 FINANCIAL ADVANTAGES OF SAUSAGE-LINK DESIGN

| | Sausage-Link Course | | Parallel Fairway Course | | Additional |
	Possible No. of Units	Premium Income	Possible No. of Units	Premium Income	Premium Bonus
Detached houses (100-ft. lots)	300	$6,000,000	80	$1,600,000	$4,400,000
Townhouses (38-ft. width	789	$15,780,000	210	$4,200,000	$11,580,000
Three-story garden apts. (40 units of frontage per 1,000 feet	1,200	$24,000,000	320	$6,400,000	$17,600,000

Source: Frederick D. Jarvis, *Land Development* (Summer 1989).

FIGURE 12.2 GOLF COURSE DESIGN OPTIONS (18-hole regulation course)

Design Options	Configuration	Land Consumption	Frontage Opportunities	Flexibility Capacity	Maintenance Cost	"Integrity"	Comments
Core		Low	Low	Low	Low	High	Oldest type, usually least expensive to build, most economical to maintain
Single fairway Continuous		High	High	Low	High	Low	Most land-consumptive but greatest amount of development frontage. Can adapt most easily to difficult sites.
Single fairway Returning nines		High (200 Acres)	High	High	High	Low	Most flexibile for play, slightly less frontage due to concentration of tees and greens for holes 1, 9, 10, and 18.
Double Fairway Continuous		Medium	Medium	Low	Medium	Medium	40% less frontage for development sites; can result in boring course design.
Double fairway Returning nines		Medium	Medium	High	Medium	Medium	Second most economical to maintain. Can usually accommodate taller buildings along the fairways.

Source: Frederick D. Jarvis "Golf: A Driving Force in Today's Real Estate Market" *Land Development* (Summer 1989), 10–15

Lot Premiums

It is commonly believed that the residential site premiums derived from a GCC can offset the cost of the land required for the course. However, there are so many variables involved that a generalization such as this should not be given serious consideration. The size of the GCC is important; small projects are at a disadvantage in this regard. The disadvantage of large projects is that they may incur compounded holding costs if they have extended absorption periods. One key to success is the project's ability to support increasing lot values throughout the initial marketing program. The amenities of a country club should broaden the potential market for the lots by appealing to a wider range of demographic groups.

These considerations are attractive to developers, but success is not guaranteed, especially if supply and demand factors are unfavorable. Lot premiums are highly variable and depend on the visual quality of the layout. Premiums can range from 40% to 75%, and average approximately 50%. Appraisers and analysts should base their estimates on the results achieved at competitive projects over the same time frame and in the same market area. The historical performance of nearby projects may not be relevant due to changing market dynamics.

Developers should resist the temptation to place houses at every possible location on both sides of the fairway. Maximizing residential development along fairways can wall off the golf course and make it difficult to sell the residences without frontage. When a course lacks visibility, it cannot be said to provide community open space. Architects and designers have recognized the need to extend golf course amenities throughout a GCC.

Windows and Focals

A land planning technique developed by David Jensen Associates extends golf course premiums to nonfrontage lots by creating open space "windows" through which residents can see the golf course.[2] Higher lot prices are promoted by increasing the number of focals or "hot spots" on the course.

In the design shown in Figure 12.3, local interior roads and cul-de-sacs are run through these windows into the interior lots giving many of the homes on the cul-de-sac views of the golf course. Lots situated across the road are considered to have secondary frontage on the course.

Lots with golf views do not command prices equal to those obtained for

2. David Jensen "Windows and Focals," *Urban Land* (August 1990), 26–29.

FIGURE 12.3

TRADITIONAL LOT PATTERN

In the typical layout of golf course communities, interior lots can be walled off from the golf course.

WINDOWS

Creating windows with views of the course and developing roads through them gives residents the feel of truly living in a golf community.

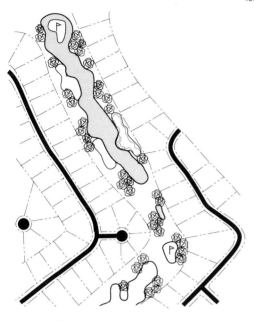

Source: David Jensen Associates

FIGURE 12.4

CREATE HOT SPOTS

Greens, tees, lakes, traps, and first-shot landing areas are the typical hot spots of a golf course. More prime lots can be created by placing additional attractive views—of ponds, streams, dramatic sand traps, and wooded areas—in dead fairway areas.

HOT SPOT ORIENTATION

Good lot configuration and home siting can maximize golf course views and thereby yield higher prices for lots. Tees, like the ones at the top and bottom, can be improved in appearance with sculpturing and flower beds.

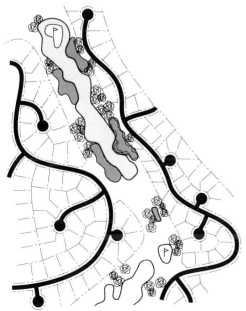

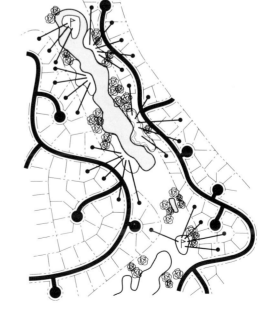

Source: David Jensen Associates

lots with frontage on the course and all frontage is not uniform in value. The most sought-after lots overlook the greens, tees, lakes, bunkers, and first-shot landing areas. Recognizing this factor, a creative developer can create additional "hot spots" or space the hot spots in a way that reduces the number of lots with standard fairway views. (See Figure 12.4.)

Creative planning is cost effective if it is based on sound design principles. The quality of the design will have a major impact on the project's financial feasibility. According to Jensen, windows and focals that maximize the exposure of lots to the golf course can improve project performance by 25% to 35%.[3]

MEMBERSHIP ARRANGEMENTS

Equal in importance to the design and layout of the GCC are the types of membership that are established and the rights to which members are entitled. There are no clearly recognized principles for deriving membership structures. A structure that is successful in one location may be less acceptable in another. Some analysts believe that the trend of popularity is moving away from private clubs and toward partial daily-fee or semiprivate arrangements because of the amount of underserved demand for golf participation and the advantageous greens fees that can be charged. Others believe that a social stigma attached to public daily-fee courses is a major reason so many real estate developers decide to establish private clubs.

Control of the investment is important. A developer will want to maintain ownership of a golf course if it produces a healthy cash flow. As a stand-alone investment, a golf project can add equity to a balance sheet and prestige to the owner. On the other hand, course costs can be so high that earnings before interest barely support debt service. In this case the developer may willingly pass title to a home owner's association after absorbing losses for an extended period.

The intricacies of membership arrangements are beyond the scope of this text. The main thing to realize is that the structure established should maximize the marketing of the GCC and yet not handcuff the golf course with an inadequate revenue stream.

Flexibility is desirable in membership arrangements. At first a golf club or resort project may want to allow daily fee players to use the course to capitalize on the club's income-producing potential. Later it may be possible to limit play to private members and guests. Some arrangements provide for nonowning members, while others require that members be property owners. A prudent developer will retain a buy-back right for nonresident memberships. Many GCCs allow residents to realize the full resale potential of their residences by automatically providing membership in the country club to new buyers, even if the seller is not a member.

It has been found that as few as 20% of GCC residents play golf, but a much larger portion, say 40% to 80%, may want to be members of the country club. Therefore, it is necessary to offer a variety of membership categories, such as full privilege membership, all sports except golf membership, and social membership, which usually means access to the swimming pool and clubhouse. Using market research and competitive pricing, a developer may be able to charge monthly or annual dues and greens fees in addition to an initiation fee. Obviously, specific fee amounts depend on the demographics of a target market area, traditional fee arrangements, and the competitiveness of GCCs in the market.

3. Ibid., 28.

◀

Scottsdale Princess
Resort Hotel in
Arizona

RESORTS AND BUSINESS PARK FACILITIES

Many signature golf projects are resort oriented, where play is limited to hotel guests and golf club members. Memberships are available to residents of the GCC and to nonresidents, who are occasional users of the course. The recent practice of paying huge prices for certain trophy courses, which was described in Chapter 10, rests on the dubious assumption that very expensive private club memberships can be sold to nonresident aliens who love the game and want the prestige of membership in an exclusive facility.

Clearly the developers of expensive golf courses in resort settings expect to increase the occupancy rate of the lodging facilities and out-market competitive facilities that do not possess the golf amenity. In the late 1980s, many of these resorts, especially those in Hawaii, were sold at extremely low capitalization rates based on the perception that future values or yields would grow higher and a limit would be placed on permits for new projects.

The economic feasibility of a golf project in a resort or business part environment can be quantified by comparing the net present values of the additional net revenues to the additional net costs of adding the golf amenity. In addition to the usual golf-related revenue sources, resorts will have higher revenues from the rooms, food and beverage department, and pro shop sales. (Sales of logo products have attractive sales margins.) Business parks expect to capitalize on golf by achieving higher property values and floor area ratios, increased absorption rates, and, in some localities, lower impact fees and infrastructure costs.

RISK REDUCTION

From a planner's perspective, GCCs have many advantages (e.g., preservation of wetlands and open space, enhancement of community image, promotion of additional property tax and other taxes for the community, orderly development of large tracts of land in a systematic and attractive manner).

However, the development process can be extremely long and expensive, resulting in excessive costs and marginal profitability. Community opposition can center on a number of issues and lead to litigation and delaying tactics. Community planners' may be concerned about infrastructure extensions, traffic problems, water supply and quality issues, pesticides, and the use of gates and brick walls to create a sense of privacy. When a course is invisible to everyone except adjacent home owners, the open space argument has little impact.

From a developer's perspective, inclusion of a golf course provides a project with a pricing and sales advantage. It enlarges the potential market for a variety of residential unit types, ranging from luxury residences to townhouses and condominium apartments. Because of these advantages, a large number of projects were started in the latter half of the 1980s. A small number of these GCCs have failed and gone into foreclosure due to development errors such as inadequate market feasibility analysis and poor golf course design. Some GCCs have resulted in lawsuits, with the home owners' association bringing a class action suit against the developers. However, there are means to avoid some of these pitfalls, even in a highly competitive atmosphere.

GCCs have unique design problems due to the relationship between the golf course and adjacent housing. Golf balls can be considered small missiles, traveling at speeds of about 250 miles per hour, or 365 feet per second. With this speed and long drives of up to 250 yards, the potential for property damage is readily apparent. Trespassing is another problem when golfers enter the yards and grounds of adjacent houses searching for errant balls. While the courts have ruled that persons living in GCCs may have to suffer some damage, annoyance, and inconvenience in exchange for the enjoyment of living near a country club, there are means of minimizing conflicts.

The owner of the golf course should retain the right to alter the landscaping that borders a course to prevent golf balls from striking homes or persons on the fairway. This right should be expressly preserved without regard for how such changes will impact the views from neighboring homes or lots.

Landscape architect William R. Firth suggests design guidelines featuring uphill housing, natural buffers, slanted view corridors, variable setbacks, and proper bunker placement and hole orientation.[4] Some of his recommendations are summarized as follows:

1. Uphill housing is generally preferred because buildings are less likely to be struck by a ball. Moreover, views down into a golf course are generally better than views looking up, and valley soils are better for fairways.

2. Trees and tall shrubs provide a natural defense against errant golf balls. Dense evergreens provide the best year-round screen. Unfortunately, the more effective the screen of vegetation is, the less visible the golf course is to the residents who paid a premium to overlook it. A buffer planting program should be made an integral part of golf course construction.

3. Careful orientation of houses helps to solve the dilemma of views versus protection. If a house looks toward the green rather than straight onto the fairway, trees should be cleared along an angled corridor facing away from the path of the golf ball. (See Figure 12.5.)

4. Conditions along fairways vary immensely, and each fairway has its

4. William R. Firth, "Can Golf and Housing Get Along?" *Urban Land* (February 1990), 16–19.

FIGURE 12.5

Analyzing Golf Course
Real Estate Projects

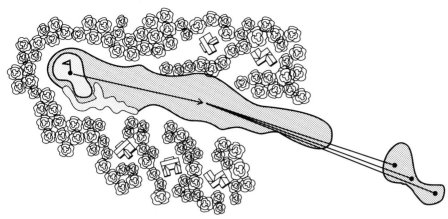

Oblique view corridors oriented away from the direction of play protect nearby homeowners while hiding surrounding houses from golfers.

Source: William R. Firth

own edge characteristics that should be considered in determining setbacks. Recognized minimum setbacks are about 70 yards from the center of the fairway to the facades of buildings, about 35 yards around tees, and about 65 yards around greens. A deep setback will be needed at a fairway edge where the drive is downhill, winds are strong, or little buffering foliage exists. A shallower setback is needed along fairways framed by dense forest.

5. In trying to avoid bunkers, many golfers drive far to their left or right and off the fairway. Bunker placement must be planned along with setbacks and buffering.

6. Golf course architects generally agree that a north-south alignment of fairways is preferable to an east-west alignment, which has early golfers playing into the morning sun and afternoon golfers playing into the setting sun. The sun's glare can affect golfers' accuracy.

Safety is a critical concern in the layout of a course within a GCC, but the architect must also be committed to golf values and playability. With the implementation of effective design principles, a golf course can be highly rated and be a good neighbor. Often the real estate component of the GCC has been the cause of the failure of the overall development. Developers must find the right balance between the demand segment of golf pricing and the housing product that will maximize market penetration. Jeffrey Maza has concluded:

> Like any niche product, GCCs involve elements of risk. The housing market is very sensitive to the general economy and quick to register a turn for the worse. Upper-end housing like that found in a golf course development is especially dependent on the trade-up market—one of the first segments to go soft in a housing slump. Should this occur, any oversupply of GCC product could take years to work off.[5]

GCC VALUATION EXAMPLE

Figure 12.6 shows a financial comparison of developing 500 acres of land with a) no golf; b) a semiprivate, daily-fee course; and c) a private equity club. Assuming there is good market potential for golf, the population's in-

5. Maza, 16.

come and other demographics are positive, and approvals can be secured, the two GCCs support higher residual land values than the unadorned subdivision project.

Some of the key assumptions in this analysis are stated below:

- On the average the daily-fee course will enhance unit lot values by about 25%, while the private course will increase lot values by 37%.
- Fairway frontage lots will have a 25%-30% premium over secondary golf view lots, a 36%-48% premium over interior lots in the GCC, and a 50%-70% premium over interior lots in the nongolf subdivision.
- The GCCs will sell out at a faster rate than the project without a golf course.

Figure 12.6 is included only to illustrate a methodology for comparing various development scenarios. The analyst should investigate the wide variety of factors that have been described in this text. A more sophisticated analytical model should be employed to prepare comparative financial and development alternatives on a net-present-value basis.

FIGURE 12.6 RESIDUAL LAND VALUE UNDER ALTERNATIVE GOLF/NO GOLF DEVELOPMENT PROGRAMS

	No Golf	Daily-Fee Golf	Private Equity Club
Development Parameters			
Land area (acres)	500	500	500
Residential	340	250	250
Golf course	—	150	150
Roads/easements/open space	160	100	100
Lots (@ 3.5/acre)	1,200	875	875
Interior	1,200	375	375
Golf view	—	200	200
Fairway frontage	—	300	300
Average improved-lot value			
Interior	$50,000	$55,000	$57,500
Golf view	—	$60,000	$65,000
Fairway frontage	—	$75,000	$85,000
Average per-unit site-improvement cost	$25,000	$28,000	$28,000
Average annual unit absorption	200	219	219
Interior	200	94	94
Golf view	—	50	50
Fairway frontage	—	75	75
Golf Parameters			
Memberships			
Golf (@ $30,000)	—	—	400
Social (@ $2,500)	—	—	250
Average memberships sold per year			
Golf	—	—	100
Social	—	—	50
Net operating income			
Year 1	—	$200,000	$400,000*
Year 2	—	$500,000	$200,000*
Year 3+	—	$750,000	—
Golf development cost (excluding land)		$6,000,000	$10,500,000
Course	—	$3,000,000	$4,000,000
Clubhouse	—	$800,000	$3,500,000
Other costs	—	$2,200,000	$3,000,000
Years to Sell Out	6.0	4.0	4.0
Cash flow projections (1990 dollars)			
Site sales	$60,000,000	$55,100,000	$60,100,000
Less: site improvement costs	$30,000,000	$24,500,000	$24,500,000
Less: other site development costs	$9,000,000	$6,000,000	$7,100,000
Net site sales	$21,000,000	$24,600,000	$28,500,000
Daily-fee asset value/membership sales†	—	$6,700,000	$11,400,000
Total cash flow	$21,000,000	$31,300,000	$39,900,000
Net present value‡ (1991 dollars)			
Net site sales	$13,600,000	$17,800,000	$20,800,000
Net daily-fee asset value/net membership sales	—	$5,800,000	$9,100,000
Total net present value	$13,600,000	$23,600,000	$29,900,000
Less: golf development costs	—	$6,000,000	$10,500,000
Residual land value	$13,600,000	$17,600,000	$19,400,000
Per acre	$27,200	$35,200	$38,800
Per unit	$11,300	$20,100	$22,200

*These values represent operating losses, or required developer subsidies, during the membership sales period.
†Represents stable year net income of $700,000 capitalized at 10.4%. Represents gross membership sales (golf and social) less an allowance for marketing, general, and administrative expenses.
‡Net present value calculated by discounting projected constant dollar annual cash flow stream at a 14% discount rate.

Source: The authors adapted this residual land value calculation for alternative development programs from data presented in an article prepared by J. Richard McElyea, Austin G. Anderson, and Gene P. Kreporian, "Golf's Real Estate Value," Urban Land (February 1991).

CHAPTER THIRTEEN

CONCLUSIONS AND TRENDS

The need for substantially more golf courses in the next decade cannot be overemphasized. Every publication dealing with the business aspects of golf facilities has commented on this issue repeatedly. The major problem, however, is not a lack of projects, but the inability to obtain financing.

In the last half of 1990, approximately 560 projects were under construction nationwide and 781 more were in the planning stage. Many will be substantially delayed due to environmental issues. Projects that are undercapitalized or lack financial commitments could also have a long wait. The strategic goal of adding one course per day through the year 2000 appears to be unreachable.

Environmental concerns have resulted in ad hoc activities to prevent the development of golf courses. Organized groups have rallied around emotional issues relating to the ecological damage caused by turf chemicals, drainage, and underground water levels and quality; the socio-political factor of exclusivity has also been targeted. These groups reject the greenbelt argument and ignore many of golf's positive contributions to the economy and the recreational needs of the populace.

To mitigate the water problem, recycling and irrigation with treated waste water will be increased. In addition, new design concepts such as "dry lakes" planted with desert flowers or other vegetation will be implemented. Modified or partial link courses may be able to satisfy the concerns of some critics, but opposition to proposed projects based on a variety of real and imagined environmental concerns can be expected to continue.

There is more bad news for golf enthusiasts. Writers contributing to popular business publications are circulating warnings about the industry, telling investors that they should beware of the boom in golf. They argue that golf projects can be overbuilt just as hotels and office buildings were in the 1980s, and that the new golfer will not play as often as the veteran player. Furthermore, the increasing cost of the sport is in conflict with the new consumer concept of financial conservatism and a recessionary, or at least sluggish economy.

Investors are being pulled in two directions. Major real estate organizations, hoping to capitalize on all the good publicity, are starting to promote specialized syndications for the development of golf courses. At the same time, prices for most projects have been inflated because of Japanese purchase activities. It can be smart to invest in golf, but not when the capitalization rates employed are based on unrealistic financial projections. Perhaps a dose of economic realism in the early 1990s will bring course prices down to meet traditional yield expectations.

It is wise to beware of investment opportunities that are exaggerated, but golf should not be treated as a fad. The sport has grown and generally flourished through the best and worst of economic times and has a core following in virtually all demographic groups.

One aspect of golf that gets little publicity is its significant impact on local and regional economies. Direct spending by golfers for equipment and playing fees totaled approximately $13 billion in 1988. Indirect spending for golf-related travel and lodging contributed another $7.8 billion to the GNP or "golf national product." A third category to be considered is spending by nongolfers on golf-related projects such as second homes and spending on advertising, promotions, tournaments, and other media services. At the national level, this figure is less than a third the size of indirect spending, or about $2.5 billion. The three categories of golf spending combined amount to more than $23 billion. Course operations and construction spending yield about half again of this amount per year, indicating a total national golf economy of $35 billion. On this basis golf is undoubtedly the most important participant sport in the country.

Golf will maintain its preeminent status in the coming years, but current development constraints are likely to increase. Private clubs may increasingly be subject to legal challenges and general economic conditions will hold down price and fee increases. To the individual golfer these factors are not of great importance and may actually increase course accessibility. On the management and development side, however, the 1990s will be a frustrating period with the tight money policy of the federal government restricting financing and economic uncertainty constraining the golf consumer.

To golf course appraisers and analysts, valuation problems will become more complicated and feasibility conclusions will be subject to an increasing number of complex variables. Forecasting core demand will not be so difficult, but factoring in the price of golf relative to other competing sports and leisure activities introduces elements of uncertainty (especially for marginal demand) in projections that extend beyond a few years. Similarly, the decline in commercial real estate inflation means that financial modeling must adjust to lower income and expense growth rates. These factors may have a long-term, beneficial impact on investment yields if the prime rate remains at a low level.

All of these developments will increase the importance of market feasibility analysis. Future projects cannot be expected to succeed based on inflationary expectations. Precise revenue estimates on a department-by-department basis must be prepared and supported by in-depth market research and direct contact with market participants, the managers of competitive facilities, and recognized experts. Attracting capital for financing will become increasingly difficult until long-term solutions to solve the budgetary crisis, unfavorable trade balance, and national debt funding are successfully implemented. Thus, opportunities for specialized lenders will continue, available loans will be costly and short-term in nature, and demands for cash flow or equity participation will persist.

Golf will generate a lot of excitement in the 1990s, and there will be abundant opportunities for professional managers. New equipment and products will continue to be introduced and television will exert its inevitable influence on nonparticipants, for better or worse. Well-planned and well-supported projects will be developed, while marginal projects will struggle and barely survive. Tight financial controls will become more and more necessary. New players will be attracted to the game by innovative teaching programs and specialized marketing promotions, and the seniors market will grow in importance as demographic charges increase percentages in older age group categories.

There is a growing demand for trained and knowledgeable appraisers and feasibility specialists in golf course development. The field has been seriously underserved since its beginnings. Appraisal organizations need to promote educational programs and additional research to provide needed statistics on market conditions, operational expenses, golf club sales, and terms of rental agreements. We hope that this text has succeeded in providing more information and generating more interest in this growing real estate specialty.

GLOSSARY

Bunker—An area of bare ground, often a depression, which is usually covered with sand.

Capacity—The total volume of play, typically measured in rounds per year, which a course may physically accommodate without regard to other factors such as waiting time and course maintenance. Capacity is constrained only by sunlight hours and weather conditions.

CC&Rs—Covenants, conditions, and restrictions. A promise between two or more parties, incorporated in a trust indenture or other formal instrument, to perform certain acts or to refrain from performing certain acts.

Course rating—The evaluation of the playing difficulty of a course compared with other rated courses. Courses are rated to provide a uniform, sound basis on which to compute handicaps.

Daily fee facility—A golf facility at which one pays a fee for each daily use.

Demand—The desire and ability to purchase or lease goods and services.

Desired rounds—The ideal, maximum number of rounds played per period or year which results in the highest volume of play while achieving other objectives such as desired course maintenance and waiting time. The number of desired rounds is usually established by the facility's management.

Draw—A stroke, usually deliberate, played across the ball from "in to out" causing it to travel at first to the right and then curve back toward the line required; a half-brother to the hook.

Driving range—A limited area of land with a line of bays or stalls from which golfers can practice shots. Golfers rent the balls, but do not have to pick them up.

Executive course—A short version of a regulation course with a par between 58 and 68 strokes.

Fade—The opposite of a draw; a shot moving slightly from left to right toward the target. A fade is usually deliberate and controlled, unlike a slice.

Fairway—The specially prepared and cut part of the course between the tee and the green. The fairway is surrounded by rough, bunkers, and other hazards.

Focals—The "hot spots" on the golf course, including greens, tees, lakes, bunkers, and first-shot landing areas which have visual characteristics that command higher lot premiums.

Focus group interview—A market research technique involving comprehensive questioning of a small group of potential consumers. The purpose of the study is to test participants' reactions to specific topics. Those interviewed are not made aware of these topics; the questioning begins on a general basis and gradually focuses to the topics. The objective of the focus group interview is to gather information; there are no correct answers.

Forecast—An individual's expectation of future performance, which may be based on projections or other relevant data and judgment as in a market forecast or financial forecast.

Former golfer—A person who has played golf in the last two years, but not in the last year.

Golf accessibility rate—The total population of a defined area expressed as the number of persons for each 18 holes.

Golf capacity utilization—The actual rounds achieved by a course divided by the number of desired rounds. A private course may prefer to express capacity utilization as the number of actual members of the club divided by the maximum number of desired members.

Golf car—A powered vehicle, usually electric, in which one or two golfers may ride and carry their equipment.

Golf cart—An unpowered hand cart for carrying golf equipment.

Golf frequency rate—The average number of rounds played per year for a defined segment of the golfing population.

Golf participation rate—The percentage of the total population in a defined area, age five and older, who have played golf at least once within the survey year.

Golf playability—The relationship between the design features of a particular layout and the talents of the golfers who will play on it.

Golf revenue multiplier (*GRM*)—A unit of comparison used in the sales comparison approach that is equal to the sale price divided by direct golf revenues (i.e., greens fees, car fees, and driving range).

Golf values—Those qualities, sometimes quite subtle, that make a layout or round of golf either a memorable experience or a forgettable one.

Golfer—One who has played golf at least once in the last year.

Greens—The whole course over which the game is played, not just the area commonly called the green, which is, strictly speaking, the putting green.

Greens fee multiplier (*GFM*)—A unit of comparison used in the sales comparison approach that is equal to the sale price divided by gross greens fee revenues (i.e., average greens fee times total annual rounds). The factor equals the price paid per dollar of greens fee.

Hazards—Any bunker or water hazard located within the course of play of a hole.

Heroic holes—Holes with a combination of penal and strategic design. Hazards are placed diagonally, and the golfer shoots accordingly. About 30% to 50% of holes are heroic.

Highest and best use—The reasonably probable and legal use of vacant land or an improved property, which is physically possible, appropriately supported, financially feasible, and results in the highest value.

Hook—A golf stroke in which the ball's flight path begins to the right of the direct line to the target and finishes to the left. For a left-hander, this is reversed.

Internal rate of return (*IRR*)—The annualized rate of return on capital that is generated or capable of being generated within an investment or portfolio over the period of ownership; similar to the equity yield rate.

The *IRR* is often used to measure profitability. It is the rate of discount that makes the net present value of an investment equal to zero.

Market segmentation—The process of identifying groups of buyers with different purchasing desires or requirements.

Municipal course—A golf course which is owned by the public, i.e., a city or county.

Net cash flow—The net operating cash flow plus proceeds of the reversion in the last year of a discounted cash flow analysis.

Net operating cash flow—The actual or anticipated net operating income less an allowance or reserve for periodic replacement of short-lived capital items, before deducting mortgage debt service or depreciation, and before reversion value.

Net operating income—The actual or anticipated net income remaining after deducting all expenses from effective gross income, but before deducting mortgage debt service, depreciation, and any allowance or reserve for the replacement of long-lived capital items.

Nongolfer—An individual who has not played golf within the last two years.

Nonproprietary facility—A golf facility that is owned by a party other than its members, who enjoy a right to use.

Par—The score an expert golfer would be expected to make for a given hole. Par means errorless play without flukes and, under ordinary weather conditions, allows for two strokes on each putting green. Par is based on the yardage recommended by various governing bodies. Par applies to each individual hole and is governed by the length of the hole, not necessarily its difficulty. Difficulty is measured as the standard scratch score in Britain and elsewhere, and the course rating in America. The standard par for an 18-hole course is 72 strokes.

Par-3 course—A course in which each hole has a par 3 rating and is less than 250 yards in length.

Penal holes—Holes in which sand traps guard the greens in bottleneck or island fashion and force the golfer to shoot accurately or play short. Penal design is usually found on one or two short holes on an 18-hole course.

Pitch-and-putt course—A small course with holes, usually less than 100 yards in length.

Price per membership (*PPM*)—A unit of comparison used in the sales comparison approach equal to the sale price divided by the number of members in the club.

Price per round (*PPR*)—A unit of comparison used in the sales comparison approach equal to the sale price divided by the number of annual rounds played.

Primary data—Information that is gathered firsthand by the researcher usually through interviews or surveys. Primary data are specific to the topic researched, which may be the subject golf course or its immediate market.

Projection—Extrapolating future events from a series of former events, often by regression analysis. A projection such as a market projection or financial projection is based solely on the former events' trend.

Proprietary facility—A golf facility in which the members share in the equity ownership.

Putting green—The specially prepared part of every golf hole where the cup is situated and the putting takes place. Ideally, greens are closely mowed, creating a smooth and fast surface.

Regulation course—A course that meets these minimum standards: length of 3,200 yards for 9 holes and 6,500 yards for 18 holes, and a par of 35 strokes for 9 holes and 72 strokes for 18 holes. Par will range from three to five strokes per hole.

Reversion value—A lump-sum benefit that an investor receives at the termination of an investment.

Roughs—The part of a golf course that is neither tee, green, fairway, nor hazard. Because roughs are unmanicured areas, play from the rough is difficult.

Round—One golfer playing 18 holes, or 9 holes on a 9-hole course.

Secondary data—Data that have been gathered by a source other than the researcher such as the U.S. Census Bureau or the National Golf Foundation. These data usually relate to macro conditions and are not specific to the subject property.

Semiprivate facility—A golf course that offers a private membership status (either proprietary or nonproprietary) and also allows daily fee use of the course to the public.

Shoulder season—The period of time between the prime season and the off season, usually in the spring and fall.

Signature golf course—A course designed by a well-recognized, acclaimed architect, which is usually distinguished by characteristics specific to that designer.

Slice—A stroke that starts to the left of the direct line to the target and finishes to the right. For a left-hander, this is reversed.

Strategic holes—About one-half the holes on a modern golf course are strategic—i.e., they have fewer traps but are well placed. The golfer can hit at full power but must place the shots.

Supply—The various amounts and types of goods or services that are available for sale at different prices.

Target market—The market segment that a particular facility is designed to serve.

Tee—1) The raised and suitably marked ground from which the player begins each hole. 2) A wooden or plastic peg on which the ball is placed for the initial shot to each hole.

Total revenue multiplier (*TRM*)—A unit of comparison used in the sales comparison approach equal to the sale price divided by total facility revenues.

Water hazard—Any sea, lake, pond, or other open water course within the area of play.

Windows—Open areas on the perimeter of the golf course that provide direct views of the golf course.

RESULTS OF GOLF FACILITIES FINANCING SURVEY

A Survey of Lenders Prepared in Conjunction with *Golf Courses and Country Clubs: A Guide to Appraisal, Market Analysis, Development, and Financing*

Q-1) Please indicate your type of lending institution: (Check only one)

RANKING
- (1) Commercial Bank
- (2) Savings Institution
- ( ) Insurance Company
- ( ) Mortgage Banker
- (4) Asset-Based Lender
- (5) Investment Banker
- ( ) Pension Fund
- (3) Other: mortgage broker, credit corporation, consultant broker

Q-2) Please note the geographic locations served by your institution: (Check all that apply)

RANKING
- (2) Nationwide
- (4) Northeast
- (5) Central Atlantic
- (1) Southeast
- (8) Midwest
- (9) Gulf States
- (6) Southwest
- (7) Northwest
- (3) Outside Continental U.S. (Hawaii)

Q-3) Please indicate the size of your institution in total assets: (Check only one)

RANKING
- (4) Under $500 million
- (1) $500 million to $2 billion
- ( ) $2 billion to $5 billion
- ( ) $5 billion to $10 billion
- ( ) $10 billion to $25 billion
- (2) over $25 billion

Q-4) Please check the types of golf and golf-related projects and properties your institution is willing to consider for a loan: (Check all that apply)

RANKING

(7) 9-hole golf course, public play
(1) 18-hole golf course, public play
(4) 18-hole golf course, private play only
(2) 18-hole golf course, private & public play
(5) Country club with golf course
(9) Country club without golf course
(6) Golf resort, with hotel and private club
(8) Golf & tennis resort, hotel, private club
(3) Residential development with golf course & private club

Q-5) Please indicate the number and type of golf-related projects and properties your institution has financed in the past five years:

Example: (11) 9-hole golf course, public play
(Eleven loans made on 9-hole courses in the past 5 years)

RANKING AND PERCENT		
( ) 9-hole golf course, public play	NONE
(1) 18-hole golf course, public play	35%
(7) 18-hole golf course, private play only	1%
(3) 18-hole golf course, private & public play	13%
(4) Country club with golf course	12%
( ) Country club without golf course	NONE
(5) Golf resort, with hotel and private club	4%
(6) Golf & tennis resort, hotel, private club	3%
(2) Residential development with golf course and private club	32%

Q-6) Please indicate the permissible use of loan proceeds for golf-related projects and properties your institution is willing to consider lending to: (Check all that apply)

RANKING

(1) Development financing for construction
(5) Initial take-out financing, upon completion of construction
(2) Refinancing
(3) Expansion or renovation
(4) Bridge financing for acquisition

Q-7) Please indicate the type of loan you would consider (or require) for a golf-related property: (Check all that apply)

RANKING

(5) Fixed-term, fully amortizing
(2) Fixed-term, partial amortization with balloon
(3) Variable interest rate
(4) Short-term only (5 years or less)
(1) Short-term, construction only

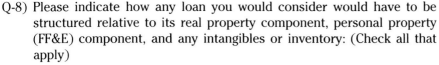

Q-8) Please indicate how any loan you would consider would have to be structured relative to its real property component, personal property (FF&E) component, and any intangibles or inventory: (Check all that apply)

RANKING

(4) Real property, FF&E, intangibles, and inventory under one loan and set of loan terms

(3) Separate loan and loan terms for real property and FF&E

(2) No loans made for intangibles and inventory

(5) Loan policy regarding allocation between real and personal property is rigid.

(1) Loan policy regarding allocation between real and personal property is flexible and may vary.

Q-9) Typical loan requirements summary: (Please enter answers in ranges.) Please assume a conventional first mortgage, not a construction loan.

MEANS AND RANGES

(58 to 73) Loan-to-value ratio (loan amount/total value, real property/FFE/intangibles)   Max = 50 to 80

(1.15 to 1.28) Debt service coverage ratio (cash flow before depreciation & taxes/annual loan debt service)   Max = 1.0 to 1.5

(160 to 460) Loan interest rate range (basis points over prime interest rate)   Max = 0 to 500

(70 to 85) Loan-to-cost ratio (loan amount/total cost of collateral)   Max = 50 to 100

(1.00 to 2.25) Loan placement/ origination fee (loan origination fee as a percentage of loan amount)   Max = .75 to 3.5

(20 to 25) Typical amortization term (Most common loan term in years, months)   Max = 10 to 30

(1.15 to 5) Borrower total net worth (as a multiplier of loan amount)   Max = 1 to 10

Q-10) Do your responses to Question Q-9 above change significantly depending on the use of loan proceeds or the terms of the loan agreement?

RANKING

(2) Loan requirements do not vary much based upon the use of loan proceeds.

(1) Loan requirements can vary significantly based upon the use of loan proceeds.

( ) Construction loans typically have an interest rate which is 85 to 165 basis points above a non-construction loan.

Q-11) Within your organizational structure, would a permanent loan to a golf-related facility be considered a "real estate" loan or an "operating" or "commercial" loan?

RANKING &
PERCENT
(1) Real estate loan, administered by real estate loan officer   70%

(2) Commercial or operating loan administered by commercial loan department   30%

Q-12) Key ratios/criteria for evaluating loan applications
Please rank in order of importance each category from 1 to 7 in terms of their importance in evaluating a golf facilities loan application:
1 = most important; 7 = least important

RANKING
(3) Loan-to-value ratio

(1) Debt service coverage ratio

(5) Pro forma current ratio of owning entity after commencement of operations

(6) Pro forma quick ratio of owning entity after commencement of operations

(4) Project market share, as a percentage of total market area (e.g. number of rounds played, etc.)

(2) Loan-to-cost ratio

(7) Other ratio/relationship: credit of sponsor; other profit potentials

Q-13) What is the minimum and maximum loan amounts for a golf-related property your institution will consider?

MEANS AND Minimum: ($1,000,000) Range $50,000 − $3,000,000
RANGES   Maximum: ($12,000,000) Range $4,000,000 − $25,000,000

Q-14) Would you require outside professional golf course and clubhouse management when financing a proposed golf course facility? (Check only one)

RANKING & (1) Yes   70%
PERCENT (2) No   30%

Q-15) To what extent will the borrower's track record in golf course and clubhouse management affect your requirements for outside management?

RANKING
(3) No effect; require outside management for all new projects.

(2) Some effect; strong management track record by developer is okay.

(1) Significant effect; management of proposed facilities reviewed on a case-by-case basis.

Q-16) Would you consider lending to a mixed-use project, with golf or golf-related facilities as one of several components:

RANKING & 90% (1) Yes
PERCENT 10% (2) No − Go to Question Q-18

Q-17) Please list the categories of mixed-use facilities you would consider lending to:

RANKING
(1) Golf course with single-family residential homesites

(2) Golf course with residential lots and resort hotel

(3) Golf course with resort hotel only

(4) Golf course with income property, timeshare (list other development components)

Q-18) In such a mixed-use project, would the financing provided to the golf course be segregated from the other use components by having a separate loan amount, loan term, interest rate, or loan documentation?

RANKING   (2) Yes
                    (1) No

Q-18a) For a mixed-use project, please cite the optimum range of project cost or value attributed to the golf course and its related improvements: (Percentage of total project value or cost that golf facilities comprise)

MEAN AND   (20% to 40%) Maximum = 10% to 70%
RANGE

Q-19) Do you have a different lending criteria for loans to either new or established country clubs which operate a golf course as opposed to a dedicated golf facility only? (A country club will have food, beverage, and banquet facilities, as well as tennis and other sporting activities.)

RANKING &   (2) Yes − 20%
PERCENT   (1) No − 80%

Q-20) Does your institution solicit owners and developers of golf-related properties as financing customers?

RANKING   (1) Yes
                    (2) No

Q-21) Please list the ways your institution solicits financing customers for golf-related properties? (Check all that apply)

RANKING   (3) Institutional advertising
                    (1) Word of mouth
                    (2) Participation in golf seminars
                    (5) Participation in lender lists in publications
                    (4) Use of correspondence
                    (6) Other: broker network (Please list)

Q-22) Do you and your institution perceive golf and golf-related facilities financing as a growth area in the next five years?

RANKING &   (1) Yes − 100%
PERCENT   ( ) No −

Q-23) Please list those reasons why financing of golf and golf-related facilities represents a growth area for your institution: (Check all that apply)

RANKING   (1) Growth in number of players/player demand
                    (2) Opportunity necessitated by overbuilt markets for other types of income properties
                    (3) Continued interest by foreign investors/purchasers in golf properties
                    (4) Opportunity for higher interest rate yield than provided by other types of income properties
                    (5) Other: alternative use of land; opportunity for conservative underwriting (Please list.)

COMPARATIVE EXPENSE RATIOS

REVENUES AND OPERATIONAL EXPENSE RATIOS
SEVEN CATEGORIES OF COURSE OWNERSHIP
PERCENTAGE DISTRIBUTION BY DEPARTMENT, 1989

	Private Equity	Private Nonequity	Semi-private	Municipal	County or State	Military	University
Income							
Greens fees	16.2	21.0	35.1	39.3	39.9	27.1	38.7
Golf cars	23.4	22.2	21.6	18.8	19.5	13.3	19.4
Golf range	3.6	3.5	3.9	5.8	4.3	2.4	4.3
Pro shop services	4.3	2.1	1.9	2.0	3.0	—	1.1
Golf lessons	1.4	1.2	0.8	0.9	0.7	0.8	1.0
Club repair	1.0	0.8	0.5	0.6	0.6	0.7	0.7
Club rentals	0.3	0.5	0.8	0.6	0.4	1.0	0.6
Food & beverage	15.0	16.8	13.5	11.6	12.0	18.1	7.5
Merchandise sales	28.5	26.1	15.8	15.3	14.5	28.9	19.8
Tournaments	3.2	3.2	2.6	2.1	1.6	3.3	3.9
Misc. income	3.1	2.6	3.5	3.0	3.5	4.4	3.0
Total	100%	100%	100%	100%	100%	100%	100%
Expenses							
Payroll & expense	15.2	19.0	20.5	17.1	20.0	36.6	29.5
Insurance	2.0	2.8	2.9	2.6	2.2	1.2	0.9
Office expenses	2.8	1.6	1.7	1.5	0.7	3.0	0.9
Golf car	3.2	4.2	2.8	2.4	3.8	3.5	2.9
Range	1.0	0.9	0.8	1.0	1.0	1.5	1.5
Club repairs	0.4	0.4	0.3	0.3	0.4	0.7	
Food & beverage	10.0	12.2	7.7	6.3	4.4	13.0	2.9
Utilities	3.1	4.2	2.8	2.9	2.6	4.6	2.2
Phone	0.4	0.5	0.5	0.3	0.4	0.3	0.4
Postage	0.2	0.3	0.2	0.1	0.1	0.1	0.2
Tournaments	0.6	0.5	0.4	0.4	0.4	0.4	0.5
Account/legal	0.5	0.6	0.5	0.5	0.4	0.7	0.6
Dues/subscription	0.1	0.1	0.1	0.1	0.1	0.1	0.1
Employee benefits	1.2	1.5	1.3	1.3	1.9	2.4	1.9
Automobile	0.6	0.5	0.5	0.4	0.5	0.4	0.4
Misc.	0.8	0.9	0.9	0.7	0.8	1.1	1.1
TOTAL	42.1	50.2	43.9	37.9	39.7	69.6	46.4

Source: Professional Golfers' Association
Note: Course maintenance costs and property taxes were not included in this survey and tabulation.

REGIONS USED IN SUPPLY AND DEMAND ANALYSIS
(See Chapter 4.)

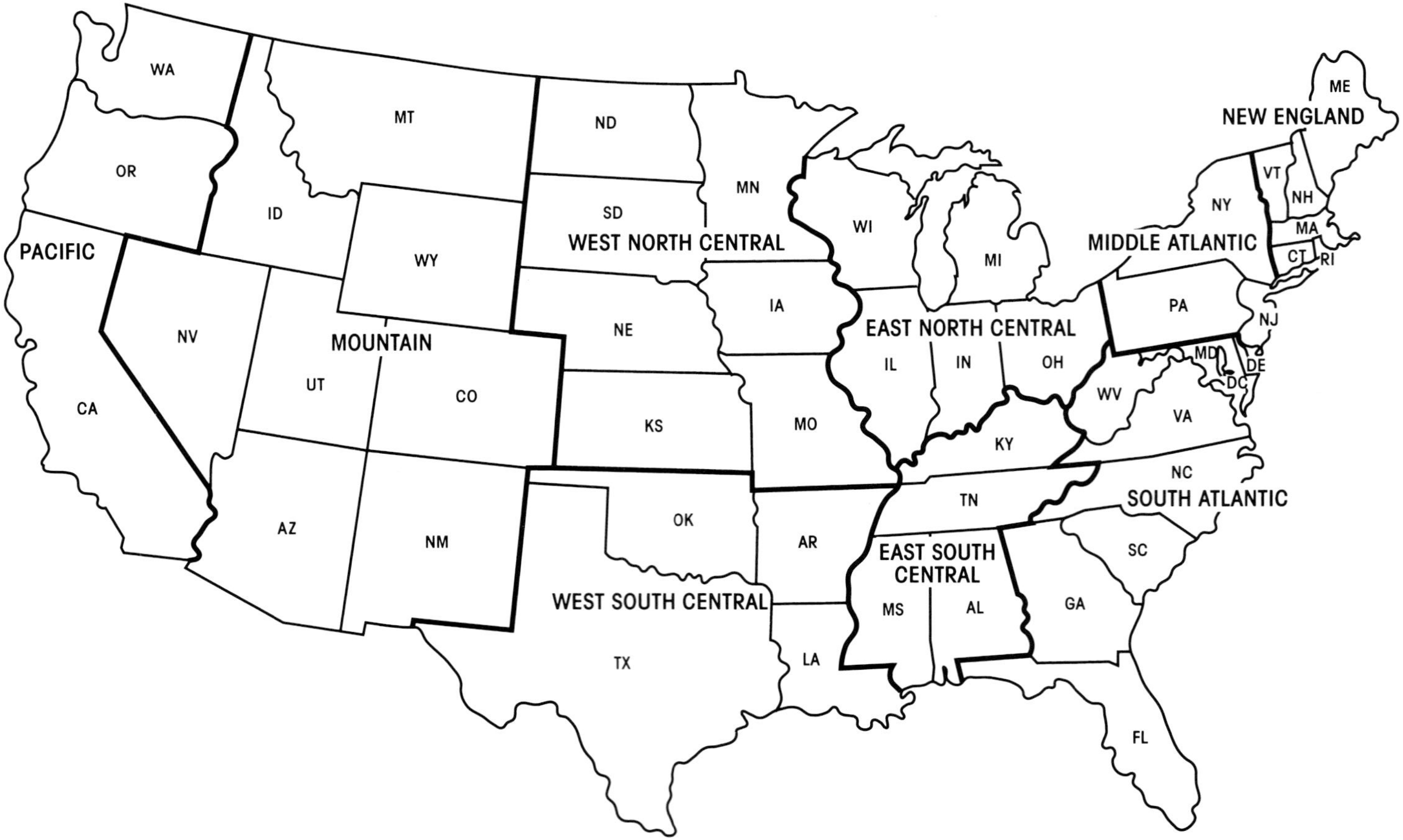

SAMPLE INVENTORY OF FF&E

Golf Shop and Office

Quantity	Item
1	Scotsman mobil golf shop
1	National Guardian alarm system
2	Data Checker cash register, model 311190
3	6-button Spirit phones
3	Stacking chairs
1	Stacking chairs
1	Oak coffee table
1	Oak credenza
1	Walnut desk
1	Swivel arm chair
1	Side arm chair
1	Stacking chairs
1	Oak bookcase
1	Minolta copier
1	Credit card authorization terminals
1	Farrington credit card slide imprinter
5	Motorola chargers
5	Motorola radius P10D portable two-way radios
1	National Guardian alarm system
1	AT&T Spirit phone system
2	24-button Spirit phone system
3	6-button Spirit phones
1	EM PAC PC 40 meg. hard drive 3604242
1	Panasonic printer #KK – P1092
1	Casper monitor #LC A 38019786
1	2-door storage cabinet – putty color
1	Legal-size file cabinet – putty color
2	Letter-size file cabinets – beige color
1	Chair mat
2	End tables
4	Game chairs
1	Game table
1	Refrigerator
3	Lamps
1	Lateral file
1	Loveseat
1	Oak desk
1	Oak credenza
3	Side arm chairs
1	Sofa
3	Stacking chairs
2	Swivel arm chairs
3	Typing chairs
1	Sharp Z-10 copier

2	Steel desks	
1	Glass-top drafting table	
Subtotal		$ 89,000

Maintenance and Shop Equipment

Quantity	Item
1	Ford Ranger XLT Super truck
1	Sandkat Vicon tractor
1	Vicon speed spreader
1	Ford 1971 backhoe and skip loader
1	Ditch Witch 2300 trencher
1	Ditch Witch 350 SXD trencher
1	John Deere 1050 tractor
1	Ford 3600 tractor
1	Flail mower
1	Brush hog disc
1	Kawasaki all-terrain vehicle
1	Kawasaki all-terrain vehicle
1	John Deere utility vehicle
1	John Deere utility vehicle
1	Sandberg compressor
1	Post drill press
1	Grossman trailer
1	Grossman trailer
1	Grossman trailer
1	Grossman trailer
1	John Deere broom
1	Tripac aerator
1	John Deere frontline mower
1	Florida Turf/JAC greens mower
1	Homelite UTO1551
1	Airleasco 163–002H pressure washer
1	Ingram box scrapper
1	Foley grinder model #388
1	Western Range ball washer
1	Carryall II with cage
1	Brower sod cutter Mark II
1	Brower turf roller
1	John Deere generator
1	Igram York rake
3	John Deere push mowers
3	John Deere 450 G trimmers
1	5-Gang EZ – picker
1	John Deere skid loader
1	Howard Price 5-gang mower
1	John Deere rotary tiller
4	Jacobsen mowers w/wheels
1	Jacobsen DW224 turfcat model 72
3	National Tre-Plex mowers
1	Standard golf brush extensions
1	Turfco Met-R-Matic dresser #85415
2	Jacobsen mowers w/wheels
1	Ford rotary mower
78	Golf cars
4	Jacobsen groomers
1	Toyota dump truck
1	Cherry picker
1	Shop hand model SW100
1	Power press model #CP100
1	Steel table

2	Wood-top lunch tables
1	Chain saw
1	REMC/pro tool box
1	Green Machine #3000 trimmer
1	Green Machine #3000 trimmer
3	Green Machine #300 trimmer
3	Used gas golf cars
3	Toro verti/cut heads
1	Toro 450D 5-gang mower
1	Toro 450D 5-gang mower
1	John Deere aerator
1	Shop grinder

Subtotal $449,850

Snack Bar

Quantity	Item
1	Hot water heater
1	Intercom system
—	Telephones
1	Three-compartment sink
1	Three-compartment Silver King refrigerator
—	Towel dispensers
—	Soap dispensers
—	Mirrors
—	Television with remote control
—	Fans
—	Bar gun
—	Light fixtures
—	Makeup table with 2 benches
1	Three-compartment sink
1	Hand sink
1	Three-compartment Delfield refrigerator
1	Two-door upright Traulsen refrigerator
1	Electric grill
1	Wells french fryer
1	Hood system with ansul fire protection
1	Two-compartment Master Bilt freezer
1	Ice machine
1	Soda machine
1	Storage cabinet
1	Serving cabinet
—	Fire detectors
—	Hot water heaters

Subtotal $ 80,000

Miscellaneous

Quantity	Item
1	Lot of golf course accessories; flags, poles, cups, trash cans, trap rakes, etc.
20	Square oak tables, 36 in. x 36 in.
5	Oak coffee tables, 42 in. x 16 in.
20	Barrell chairs
80	Oak captain's chairs
1	Automatic ice maker

Subtotal $ 30,000
Grand Total $648,850

BIBLIOGRAPHY

GOLF ASSOCIATIONS

American Society of Golf Course Architects, 221 North LaSalle Street, Chicago, IL 60601

Club Managers Association of America, 1733 King Street, Alexandria, VA 22314

Golf Course Builders of America, 920 Airport Road, Suite 210, Chapel Hill, NC 27514

Golf Course Superintendents Association of America, 1421 Research Park Drive, Lawrence, KS 66049

National Club Association, 3050 "K" Street, NW, Suite 330, Washington, DC 20007

National Golf Foundation, 1150 South U.S. Highway 1, Jupiter, FL 33477

Professional Golfers' Association, 100 Avenue of the Champions, Box 109601, Palm Beach Gardens, FL 33410–9601

U.S. Golf Association, Golf House, Far Hills, NJ 07931

GOLF PERIODICALS

Golf, Times Mirror Magazines, One Park Avenue, New York, NY 10016

Golf Business & Real Estate News, Crittenden Institute, P.O. Box 6119, Novato, CA 94948.

Golf Course Development and Operations Quarterly, National Golf Foundation, 1150 South U.S. Highway 1, Jupiter, FL 33477.

Golf Course News, United Publications, Inc., P. O. Box 997, 38 Lafayette Street, Yarmouth, MN 04096.

Golf Development, Crittenden Institute, P.O. Box 6119, Novato, CA 94948.

Golf & Grounds, Resort Publishers, Inc., Route 12, Box 497, Crossville, TN 38555.

Golf Industry, Sterling Southeast, Inc., 3230 W. Commercial Blvd., Suite 250, Fort Lauderdale, FL 33309.

Golf Market Today, National Golf Foundation, 1150 South U.S. Highway 1, Jupiter, FL 33477.

Articles

Adams, Robert L.A. and John F. Rooney, Jr. "Evolution of American Golf Facilities," *Geographical Review*, vol. 75, no. 4 (October 1985) American Geographic Society of New York.

Bechtel, Al. "Courses in Industrial and Office Park Environments," *Development Magazine* (July/August 1989): 214.

Bowden, Ralph S. "Residential Amenities: Long-Term Lessons Lead to Long-Term Financial Planning," *Urban Land* (October 1985): 36–37.

Firth, William R. "Can Golf & Housing Get Along?" *Urban Land* (February 1990): 16–19.

Jarvis, Frederick, "Golf: A Driving Force in Today's Real Estate Market," *Land Development* (Summer 1989): 10–15.

Maza, Jeffrey, "Golf & Development – A Profitable Match," *Real Estate Report*, vol. 18, no. 6: 13–16.

McElyea, J. Richard and Gene P. Krikorian, "The Changing Economics of Golf," *Urban Land* (January 1987): 12–16.

Minter, Nancy L. "Golf Course Development," *Urban Land* (November 1988): 40.

Poellot, Michael, "Tight Land & Golf," *Urban Land* (November 1990): 12–15.

Townsley, William J. "Valuation of Golf Courses," *Property Tax Journal* (September 1985): 161–195.

"Update of Golf Economics," *Urban Land* (September 1990): 26–27.

"A Village Centered on a Golf Course," *Urban Land* (October 1989): 28–29.

"Windows & Focals," *Urban Land* (August 1990): 26–29.

"Golf Courses: Hot Investment For The 90's," *Investor Outlook* (October 1990).

"Sculpture Enhances Golf Courses & Sells Homes," *Professional Builder* (March 1988): 94.

BOOKS

Phillips, Patrick, *Developing With Recreational Amenities: Golf, Tennis, Skiing & Marinas*. Washington, D.C.: Urban Land Institute, 1986.

Strawn, John. *Driving the Green*. New York: Harper Collins, 1991.

Urban Land Institute, *Golf Course Communities: Residential Communities That Are Golf-Oriented*, Washington, D.C.: Urban Land Institute. (Compilation of *Project Reference File* case studies originally published between 1978 to 1983.)

National Golf Foundation Publications

Americans' Attitudes Toward Golf in Their Community (MR004), 1991.

Buying or Leasing a Golf Course (GCP04) (Published by the Professional Golfers' Association, December 1989, and available through the National Golf Foundation.)

The Consumer's Cost of Golf (MR007), 1991.

Golf Consumer Profile, 1989 Edition (RPO68), August 1989.

Golf Course Design and Construction (GCP01), 1990.

Golf Course Maintenance Report, 87 Edition (RP007), August 1987.

Golf Courses Operation Survey, 86 Edition (RP003), June 1986.

Golf Facilities in the United States, 1991 Edition (RP021), March 1989.

Golf Participation in the United States, 1991 Edition (RP001), June 1991.

Golf Travel (MR001), 1991.

Guidelines for Planning and Developing a Public Golf Course (GCP17), 1989.

Guidelines for Planning, Building & Operating a Golf Range (GCP16), August 1990.

Mitigating & Regulating Development Impacts (GCP23) (Published by the Urban Land Institute, 1990, and available through the National Golf Foundation.)

Planning and Developing a Golf Range Complex (CGP13), January 1990.

Planning the Golf Clubhouse (GCP02), 1986.

Stand-Alone Golf Ranges in the U.S. (MR603), 1991.

Trends in the Golf Industry (MR001), 1991.

Women in Golf (MR005), 1991.

INDEX